中文教学手册：
任务型教学活动与评量
（中）

Published by Phoenix Tree Publishing Inc.

Copyright © 2021 Miao-fen Tseng & Yan Gao

ALL RIGHTS RESERVED

Not Part of this book covered by the copyright hereon may be reproduced or used in any form or by any means – graphic, electronic, including photocopying, taping, web distribution, information storage, and retrieval system, or in any other manner, without prior written permission from the publisher.

Phoenix Tree Publishing Inc. has the exclusive right of the general distribution of this publication across the world.

A Handbook of Tasks and Rubrics for Teaching Mandarin Chinese (Volume 2)

By Miao-fen Tseng

ISBN: 978-1-62575-312-0

Library of Congress Control Number: 2014954012

First Printing: October 2020

Printed in the US

Editors: Yao Li, Chao Shi

Phoenix Tree Publishing Inc.

5660 North Jersey Ave, Chicago, IL 60659

Phone: 773.250.0707 Fax: 773.250.0808

Email: marketing@phoenixtree.com

For information about the special discounts for bulk purchases,

Please contact the publisher at the address above.

Find out more about Phoenix Tree Publishing Inc. at

www.phoenixtree.com

Preface

It has been six years since the first volume of this series was published. In those years, I was deeply immersed in research projects in Mandarin Chinese and pursuing initiatives in other world languages at my home institution. This left little time or energy for this second volume, although those ventures did open my eyes to new perspectives and approaches that have informed and improved this volume. At last this book is completed, and I am delighted to offer it to the many Mandarin Chinese educators who have been anticipating its release for so long.

I first became fascinated with task design and authentic materials in 2008. Since then, those two key concepts — task and authenticity — have ignited my intellectual passion and reshaped my teaching philosophy, curriculum design, and pedagogy. My explorative journey in the past two decades culminates in the writing and editing of this book, which is overwhelmingly more joyful, enlightening, and energizing than I could have imagined.

The new volumes differ from the first volume in several ways.

Volume 1 is all my own work, but the new volumes are built on the contributions of fifteen excellent secondary and postsecondary Chinese language educators. The wisdom of so many talented and thoughtful teachers surpasses that of any one person. While I was able to complete the first volume as the single author, it became impossible for me to work alone on this big volume. Task design adds complications and diversity in many aspects, and the scope of my world knowledge and experience proved too limited. New and diverse content knowledge and deep and careful study were required in order to create tasks appropriately and well. Many tasks in this volume challenged contributors to rethink their previous instructional frameworks, grasp a higher level of expertise in different disciplines or sub-disciplines, and then put it all together in a structured and coherent unit. All the contributors are designers and creators themselves, who started with fresh sparkling ideas and perspectives, and then, just as in treasure-hunting games, were full of excitement and found many surprises before unearthing the treasures. And what they produced as the final units are indeed more precious than treasures: they are priceless contributions to the field. This is true not just for the tasks themselves, but also for the task-specific rubrics and checklists that accompany each unit.

In terms of task difficulty and expected audience, Volume I is mainly composed of individual tasks that feature a single communicative mode for novice learners, with only a very limited number of tasks targeted at the intermediate-low level. That volume was designed mainly for learners of Chinese before the Advanced Placement (AP) stage, or in other words those who have not yet achieved the mid-intermediate level, according to the proficiency guidelines advocated by the American Council on the Teaching of Foreign Languages. The targeted proficiency level in Volume II, by contrast, is mostly intermediate, with several units appropriate for more advanced learners. Teachers of novice and beginning intermediate courses have found Volume I very useful. As they move to the next level of proficiency in their students, teachers will find Volume II more useful. It can be used as the main source for different types of tasks created for AP Chinese learners and equivalent, or beyond. Authentic materials become significantly more diversified than those selected for Volume I as well.

Finally, the three volumes are organized differently. In Volume I, tasks are grouped based on topic, while in the new volumes, theme is the organizing principle, in accordance with the curriculum framework of AP Chinese.

I've never felt so vitally recharged and reinvigorated in any writing and researching process as I did while preparing the new volumes. This experience inspires me to remind all readers — teachers and learners alike — of how wonderful life and work could be if it were all as transformative as the new volumes have been for me. Truly, this work elevates both spiritually and intellectually. The driving force of vitality — and many aha! moments — characterized the search for authentic materials, which was not easy and very time-consuming. But the entire search process was so full of surprises and even what felt like miracles. I and the other contributors to this volume have felt so fortunate to be able to select from among a wide variety of available materials the sources we found most appropriate in terms of age, level, content, medium, and so on. What felt like good luck was the result of many hours of hard work, but done with joy throughout and with many wonderful discoveries along the way.

Each unit has undergone many rounds of revision through phone and face-to-face discussions, and these discussions made the final version of this volume possible. I have found such interactions helpful and inspiring, as well-designed tasks can never be created by only a single person. Without clear guidelines, tasks can go nowhere and begin to feel disconnected and incoherent. It was crucial to do several rounds of revision and fine-tuning for each unit, although of course perfection is impossible. I found the time spent on this developmental work to be well invested. The process has been so enjoyable. Unlike research projects, which have a set sequence of steps and expected outcomes, task design invites contributors to think creatively, even to leave their comfort zones and challenge their limits — to no longer be confined to what they are used to do, think, and teach. This is what makes the process so engaging, exciting, and vital.

The new volumes include a total of twenty-eight units that are grouped into six themes according to their focus, scope, content, and objectives. As in Volume I, the first chapter lists principles and recommended strategies for implementing tasks and accompanying rubrics in classes. Each of the next six chapters (chapters two through seven) contains task-based units representing one of the six themes, while referring and connecting to each other. As users read through the instructional flow of each unit, they will find the mention of technology tools and applications that are used to complete different types of tasks in each chapter. Chapter eight therefore is added to provide an introduction to the technology applications and tools that are incorporated in different chapters.

The six thematic chapters were contributed by fifteen excellent Chinese language educators in the United States. I'm truly thankful to them for their willingness to participate in this endeavor. All of them have received training in workshops that I presented, have worked with me to co-teach courses at the University of Virginia (UVA), or co-train teachers at UVA STARTALK. They are workshop participants, STARTALK attendees, or supporting instructors and trainers in some sense; they have worked with me for as short a time as a week or as long as several years.

Luoyi Cai and Shuishui Long co-taught different levels of courses with me at UVA, and afterward worked with me on published papers before contributing units to this book. Since 2017, Dr. Yan Gao has served as a co-trainer and technology coordinator for the STARTALK combination program that I have directed at UVA since 2008. Daphne Monroy, Ya-Ching Hsu-Kelkis, Luoyi Cai, and Crystal Hsia participated in UVA STARTALK as Teaching Fellows in different years. All four returned to the program in leadership positions, the first three as practicum facilitators, and the last as a student coordinator. Lee-Mei Chen was the leading instructor of a STARTALK student program and received training from me for a couple of years. At my request, she created a video on AP Chinese 5+, which I have had the privilege to share with numerous AP Chinese teachers nationwide; the video offers valuable strategies and tips for helping students to become higher achievers. The following teachers participated in AP Chinese summer institutes that I taught in different regions. The units that they created during the workshops were revised and expanded under my guidance in preparation for inclusion in this book. The teacher trainees include Dr. Hui Chen, James Jones, Jennifer Yu Lezzi, Zhenyan Li, Jiang Shi, Huichee Yeh, Hsienyu Yu, and Yajie Zhang (in alphabetical order).

I'm especially grateful to the following Chinese educators for their contributions to editorial work. Dr. Ziyi Geng, my colleague at UVA, worked for numerous hours to edit both English and Chinese and to ensure the clarity of the instructional procedure. Annie Yan Li, who teaches Mandarin Chinese at Crescent School in Toronto, Canada, volunteered to work on the second round of editing, mainly in English, to make sure the English counterpart corresponds well to the Chinese. Finally, my heartfelt thanks to the editors at Phoenix Tree Publishing Inc., who worked together to polish the content and format and make the new volumes more user-friendly for Chinese language educators.

We are proud and grateful to present this handbook to the many passionate and devoted Chinese language educators. We trust that you will find this book to be a meaningful, truly communicative resource, and that you can take full advantage of the opportunities it offers you to connect authentic real-life experience with learners. Enjoy the exploratory journey in your task-based classrooms!

Miao-fen Tseng
At the University of Virginia

About the Author

Dr. Miao-fen Tseng is the Daniels Family NEH Distinguished Teaching Professor and the Inaugural Director of the Institute of World Languages at the University of Virginia (UVA). She has frequently given talks and workshops on Chinese language pedagogy and taught graduate-level courses under the auspices of various collaborative initiatives and professional development programs in the US and globally. Her influential roles include, but are not limited to, Director of UVA STARTALK Teacher/Student Academy, Founder and President of the Chinese

Miao-fen Tseng 曾妙芬

Language Teachers Association of Virginia (CLTA-VA), member of the CLTA Board of Directors, member of STARTALK Task Force, College Board consultant in AP Chinese, Academic Advisor and Senior Reviewer for AP Chinese Audit, and Evaluator of K-16 Chinese language programs and teacher preparation programs. She has received many accolades in recognition of her contribution to Chinese language education, among them the Albert Nelson Marquis Who's Who Lifetime Achievement Award (2019), the STARTALK Award (2008-2019), the Distinguished Alumni Award from the University of Taipei (2018), the Jefferson Trust Award (2018), the Helen Warriner-Burke FLAVA Distinguished Service Award (2016), and the Jiede Empirical Research grant (2015) by CLTA. She has written numerous peer-reviewed articles and five books, including *AP Chinese Language and Culture Teacher's Guide*, *Promoting Professionalism in Teaching AP Chinese*, and *The Handbook of Tasks and Rubrics for Teaching Mandarin Chinese* (Volume I, II, III). Her major interest lies in CFL curriculum design and pedagogy, task-based teaching, teacher training, and online teaching and technology.

曾妙芬博士目前为美国国家人文学科 Daniels Family 杰出教学教授暨弗吉尼亚大学世界外语中心创办主任，她经常受邀参与海内外演讲及中文教学工作坊，并提供各类中文专业师资培训，担任研究所创新计划课程的教授。她在中文教学界也扮演着具有影响力的角色,例如曾任美国星谈中文教师培训与学生项目主任,弗吉尼亚州中文教师学会创始人暨会长,全美中文教师学会董事,星谈线上教学筹备委员,大学理事会 AP 中文顾问,AP 中文课程审查资深学术顾问与评审委员,以及 K-16 中文语言项目与师资培养项目评鉴委员。她曾荣获诸多奖项,包括 Albert Nelson Marquis Who's Who 终身成就奖(2019),星谈联邦政府经费(2008—2019),台北市立大学杰出校友奖(2018),Helen Warriner-Burke FLAVA 杰出外语贡献奖(2016),全美中文教师学会 Jiede 实证研究奖(2015)。她的学术论文刊登在诸多专业学术期刊并出版五本专业书籍,包括《推动专业化的AP中文教学》《AP中文教学指引》《中文教学手册:任务型教学活动与评量手册(1-3 册)》。其研究领域主要为对外汉语课程设计与教学、任务型教学法、师资培训、线上教学与科技应用等方面。

About the Contributors

Luoyi Cai is an assistant professor in Chinese at the Department of Asian Studies in the University of North Carolina at Chapel Hill. Before joining the faculty at UNC in 2015, she was invited in 2013 to the University of Virginia as a visiting scholar, and in 2014, she worked as a Chinese instructor at the Chinese Summer School of Middlebury College. In addition, she taught various levels of Chinese courses in study-abroad programs including the CET-in-Shanghai Program, the UVA-in-Shanghai Summer Intensive Language Program, and the Critical Language Scholarship Program. Her research interests focus on task-supported and topic-oriented teaching pedagogies, curriculum design of Chinese Language across Curriculum (LAC), and integrating film and documentaries in intermediate and advanced Chinese language courses. Cai also serves on the board of the Chinese Language Teachers Association of North Carolina (CLTA-NC) and as the core member of CLTA Special Interest Group (SIG) of the Chinese Language Film Education Exchange. Since 2018, she has served as the practicum facilitator for the STARTALK summer programs at the University of Virginia.

Dr. Hui Chen earned her master's degree in Educational Theory at Henan University in China. She also completed the Childhood Education preparation master program and earned a doctorate in Teaching and Curriculum at Syracuse University in the United States. She holds a New York State professional teacher certificate in Childhood Education for grades 1–6 and in Mandarin Chinese for grades 1–12. Currently she is a Chinese instructor at OHM BOCES and an adjunct lecturer at SUNY Polytechnic Institute. She has both face-to-face and video-conferencing teaching experience in the United States. Her students are from local middle schools, high schools, and universities.

Lee-Mei Chen has been an Advanced Placement Chinese instructor since 2008. She has 39 years of teaching experience at weekend Chinese heritage schools, and since 1999 has been teaching at local middle and high schools. She was the convener general of the Southern California Counsel of Chinese School (SCCCS) summer teacher workshops and spring workshops in 2015, 2017, and 2020. She has been serving as the director of the SCCCS Methodology for Chinese Language Instruction workshop since 2007, actively providing teaching consultation for Chinese teachers throughout Southern California and Nevada. She is the author of ten volumes of "Teaching Chinese Overseas" (1995; revised 2004), which won her subsidy awards from the Overseas Preparation of Chinese Language Textbook, Taiwan Overseas Chinese Affairs Committee in 1998 and 2004.

Dr. Yan Gao is the recipient of ACTFL Distant Learning Award for K–12 education in 2017. She teaches Mandarin Chinese at Henrico County Public Schools in Virginia. She has been the educational technology coordinator and cotrainer at UVA STARTALK Chinese Teacher and Student Academy since 2018. As the principal of the Central Virginia Chinese School, she has been instrumental in offering online training for Chinese teachers since 2016. She has written articles and a book chapter, "Empirical Studies of Teletandem between U.S. and Taiwan Universities," in *Teaching and Learning Chinese as a Second or Foreign Language: Emerging Trends*. Since 2011, she has been making the Chinese language curriculum "real" in the online environment by introducing telecollaboration, student blogging, curation projects, and other high-impact learning activities. She is passionate about the theory and practice of Chinese language instruction.

Crystal Hsia is the founder of Mandarin For U (Los Angeles), an online Mandarin Chinese training service for K–16 students and working professionals. She integrates instructional technologies with language teaching by exploiting various tools in different scenarios. In addition to teaching via online environments, she has implemented a decentralized classroom space when teaching face-to-face at the University of California, Davis, in 2019. Since 2017, she has served as an academic coordinator for Wah Mei Chinese school (San Francisco), applying a blended learning module for K–12 heritage learners to improve reading proficiency. She offers language activities on a regular basis for the local communities as a language ambassador for Duolingo, an online language learning tool.

Ya-Ching Hsu-Kelkis earned a master's degree in teaching Chinese as a foreign language from Middlebury College, and is currently teaching Chinese at the Chinese American International School in San Francisco. For twelve years, she has taught Chinese to K–8 learners in immersion programs in the United States. She specializes in creating an enriched Chinese immersion environment in which students enjoy learning and in which the meaningful focus is on higher-order thinking skills. She has participated in many professional development programs focused on Chinese language proficiency, assessment, and curriculum design. During the past twelve years, Ya-Ching has presented at ACTFL, CLTA, NCLC, and STARTALK conferences; she also gave a one-week workshop on immersion school teaching at National Taiwan Normal University.

Shi Jiang currently teaches Mandarin Chinese at University School in Cleveland, Ohio. She earned a bachelor's degree in English and a master's degree in Teaching Chinese to Speakers of Other Languages, both from Wuhan University. From 2014 to 2016, she taught all levels of Chinese classes at John Carroll University. She has been working on developing a K–8 Chinese language curriculum.

James Jones teaches Chinese at the Perkiomen School in Pennsburg, Pennsylvania. He has endeavored for the past ten years to make the course real by having learners of Mandarin work with boarding students from China on interviews and role-plays. He also teaches Spanish, works as the Theater Technical Director, and is a Dormitory Head.

Jennifer Yu Lezzi is a New York State professionally certified teacher in Mandarin Chinese for grades 7–12. She holds a master's in teaching from Union Graduate College. Since 2014, she has been teaching for Oneida-Herkimer-Madison BOCES in their rapidly expanding Chinese Language and Culture Initiative, which has been recognized as one of the leading programs in the country. The program offers Mandarin Chinese instruction both in the classroom and via interactive video conferencing to students at public schools across New York State, employing eight full-time teachers and serving nearly 500 students statewide. As an experienced teacher, Jennifer has been designing standards-based curriculum for the BOCES program's sequential Chinese programs, writing for New York State Regent's LOTE Exam for Mandarin Chinese, and teaching Advanced Placement Chinese Language and Culture courses.

Zhenyan Li is a Mandarin Chinese teacher at Middlesex School in Massachusetts. She has more than ten years of experience teaching Mandarin Chinese, creating curriculum, and advising youth leadership programs. She has developed successful Chinese programs and cultural exchanges at Vermont Commons School, Champlain Valley Union High School in Vermont, and Westford Academy in Massachusetts. The programs at all three schools grew to offer four levels of Chinese every semester. She teaches students from a wide range of backgrounds, from those with no exposure to Chinese to native and heritage speakers.

Shuishui Long is the lecturer in Chinese from the Department of Asian Studies at Pennsylvania State University. She earned a master's in teaching Chinese as a Foreign Language from the Hong Kong Polytechnic University. In 2015, she was invited to the University of Virginia as a visiting lecturer. She has been teaching at the Chinese Summer School of Middlebury College since 2015. Prior to coming to the United States, she also taught various levels of Chinese courses in study-abroad programs such as the UVA-in-Shanghai Summer Intensive Language Program, Washington and Lee University in Shanghai Program, and the CIEE-in-Shanghai Program.

Daphne Monroy currently works as a middle school Mandarin Chinese teacher at the Haverford School in Pennsylvania. Most recently, she was a Mandarin Chinese teacher as well as the Director of Curriculum Development and Teacher Training for the Chinese Immersion Program at Germantown Academy in Pennsylvania. Previously, she was a Mandarin Chinese teacher at William Penn Charter School in Pennsylvania. With her highly praised task-based and project-based curriculum, Ms. Monroy continues her involvement with STARTALK teacher and student programs across the country. Her design, "The Scavenger Hunt in Chinatown", was collected in the book, *A Handbook of Tasks and Rubrics for Teaching Mandarin Chinese* (Volume I), by Dr. Miao-fen Tseng. She was awarded a Master of Science in Education (M.S.Ed) in Teaching English to Speakers of Other Languages (TESOL) from the University of Pennsylvania Graduate School of Education.

Huichee Yeh is a Mandarin Chinese teacher in Roslyn, New York. She teaches Mandarin Chinese to middle school and high school students. Prior to becoming a Mandarin Chinese teacher, she worked for Nassau BOCES as an interpreter for fourteen years. She earned her master's degree in TESOL from New York University. She has also translated *Travels on My Elephant*, by Mark Shand, and the PBS documentary, *In Search of China*.

Hsienyu Yu has been teaching Chinese language for eight years. She teaches Mandarin

Chinese I, II, III, and AP at South Walton High School and Walton County Virtual School. She is passionate about education and has been incorporating technology and language learning into the classroom setting. She has gained a lot of hands-on experience and feedback from her teaching and believes in the importance of authentic materials and the value of a flipped classroom in language learning. She enjoys her interaction with students. Her Chinese club won the best homecoming float contest of 2019 by recreating scenes from the Disney movie, *Mulan*. She believes that language is a gateway to another culture, so she grasps every opportunity to promote Chinese cultures in the classroom, school, and community.

Yajie Zhang teaches Mandarin Chinese at Nichols School, a private school in Buffalo, New York. She started the Chinese program in 2007 for the upper school there. After successfully advocating for Nichols to offer Chinese in middle school, she taught in both divisions. In 2009, she established a Chinese Exchange Program at Nichols middle school, affiliated with Huazhong University of Science and Technology (HUST). For the last ten years, Chinese students from HUST have come to Nichols seven times, and Nichols students have gone to Wuhan five times. In 2011, the Nichols Chinese Program was honored with the Confucius Classroom award by the Asian Society. Zhang has offered many workshops for teachers of Chinese at the University at Buffalo's Confucius Institute as well as for local Chinese teachers. She also received the Nichols Humanity Award and 2018 Nichols Summer Travel Grant.

Contents

Chapter 1   Guidelines for Task Implementation
任务执行准则 / 1

Chapter 2   Families and Communities   家庭与社区 / 11

Unit 1: Filial Piety in New Era   孝顺的时代意义 / 11

Task 1   A Story of a Family   "家"的故事 / 11

Task 2   The "24 孝" Standards   "24孝"标准 / 12

Task 3   Is Achieving "24孝" Easy?   做到"24孝"容易吗？ / 16

Task 4   An Interview   小采访 / 19

Unit 2: Gratefulness and Filial Piety   感恩与孝顺 / 23

Task 1   Feeling Grateful   感恩的心 / 23

Task 2   *The Farewell*   《别告诉她》/ 26

Unit 3: One-Child Policy   独生子女政策 / 33

Task 1   A Survey   小调查 / 33

Task 2   Change of Slogans and One-Child Policy   从计划生育标语看政策变迁 / 35

Task 3   A Story of an Adopted Chinese Girl   一个被领养的中国女孩的故事 / 41

Task 4   From "1" to "2": Change of China's One-Child Policy   从"1"到"2"：中国独生子女政策的改变 / 42

Task 5   Mini-Documentary   微纪录片 / 45

Unit 4: Chopsticks and Family   筷子与家庭 / 47

Task 1   How to Use Chopsticks Correctly?   如何正确使用筷子？ / 47

Task 2　The Chopsticks Culture　筷子文化 / 49

Task 3　Different Meanings of the Chopsticks　筷子代表的各种意义 / 53

Chapter 3　Personal and Public Identities　个人和社群认同 / 57

Unit 1: Growing up and Happiness　成长与快乐 / 57

Task 1　Classic Poems　古诗 / 57

Task 2　Growing up Happily　快乐地成长 / 59

Task 3　Growing up and the Future　成长与未来 / 60

Unit 2: Gender Equality　男女平等 / 65

Task 1　Son Preference in China　重男轻女 / 65

Task 2　Why Do the Chinese Prefer Sons?　中国人为什么重男轻女？/ 66

Task 3　Online Survey　在线调查 / 67

Task 4　Boy or Girl: What Do People Prefer in Different Countries?　不同国家的人重男轻女还是重女轻男？/ 69

Task 5　Who Does the Housework?　谁做家务？/ 70

Task 6　Gender Equality at Workplace　职场男女平等 / 72

Task 7　Gender Inequality in the World　世界上的男女不平等情况 / 74

Unit 3: Dating for You and Me　约会你和我 / 77

Task 1　Speed Dating　闪电约会 / 77

Task 2　Online Dating　线上约会 / 81

Task 3　Face-to-Face Dating　见面约会（女孩选男孩）/ 84

Task 4　Face-to-Face Dating　见面约会（男孩选女孩）/ 85

Task 5　My Dating Experiences　我的约会经历 / 87

Chapter 4   Beauty and Esthetics   美学艺术 / 91

Unit 1: Tell the Story of an Advertisement   看广告说故事 / 91

Task 1   A McDonald's Advertisement   麦当劳广告 / 91

Task 2   Plot Discussion   故事情节讨论 / 92

Task 3   Narrate and Act the Story   故事旁白和表演 / 93

Unit 2: Bring Happiness Home   把"乐"带回家 / 97

Task 1   A Video on Chinese New Year Celebration   新春贺岁片 / 97

Task 2   Story-Telling   讲故事 / 99

Task 3   Story-Writing   写故事 / 100

Unit 3: Designing Advertisements and Posters   广告海报设计 / 101

Task 1   Beauty of Chinese Characters   认识汉字的美 / 101

Task 2   Designing Advertisements   广告设计 / 104

Task 3   Designing a Library Poster   设计图书馆宣传海报 / 106

Unit 4: Advertisements in the East and the West   东西方文化对广告的影响 / 109

Task 1   Fast Food in China and the U.S.   中美快餐店的差异 / 109

Task 2   Differences Between Chinese and U.S. Coca-Cola Advertisements   中美可口可乐广告的不同 / 113

Unit 5: My Room and Chinese Feng Shui   卧室中国风 / 117

Task 1   My Bedroom   我的房间/卧室 / 117

Task 2   What Does Color Represents?   颜色象征什么意义？ / 120

Task 3   Taboos of Bedroom Feng Shui   卧室的风水禁忌 / 126

Task 4   How to Change Bedroom Feng Shui?   如何改善卧室的风水？ / 133

Task 5   Bedroom with the Best Feng Shui   谁的卧室风水最好？ / 134

Task 6   Cultural Presentation   文化报告 / 137

Unit 6: Chinese Historical Courtyard Homes (Siheyuan)   中国的四合院 / 139

Task 1   Historical Courtyard Homes   了解古代的四合院 / 139

Task 2   Modern Courtyard Homes   现代的四合院 / 150

Task 3   Rent a Siheyuan   租个四合院 / 155

Chapter 1

Guidelines for Task Implementation

任务执行准则

Tasks are multifaceted, not monolithic. With their multimodalities in content, form, and design, tasks transform a traditional classroom into a vital, energetic, engaging experience. Each unit in the new volumes include a series of tasks, ranging from two to as many as ten. Most of the units are targeted at intermediate learners; several move toward higher proficiency. As learners grow toward solid intermediate and advanced-low levels of understanding, they also grow in resiliency and are better able to cope, both cognitively and intellectually, with different types of authentic materials and more difficult situations. The challenge and excitement of task-based learning encourages students to interact with a wide variety of authentic materials and to engage in a longer series of dynamic communicative tasks. Naturally, tasks gain versatility and complexity as language proficiency increases.

Conventional wisdom holds that task-supported teaching is more appropriate for introductory and low-level courses. This is because language teachers traditionally rely heavily on printed textbooks and long-practiced curricula. Most often, it seems, that tasks are used as supplements, not the main source of instructional materials. This is misguided, we believe. In fact, when the teacher centers a class on the task-based framework, tasks are no longer just conventional scripted exercises, and student-centeredness and authentic communication become the heart of the curriculum. Tasks with different degrees of authenticity become governing components around which to sequence and organize a course or curriculum. In this way, not only do authentic and semi-authentic materials take the place of printed exercises, but these materials, grounded in real-life contexts, bring the process of meaning negotiation that takes place in the real world into the classroom. In sum, tasks are in a vacuum without authenticity.

The following session presents guidelines for using the tasks compiled in the now volumes.

I. Select Units in Six Themes

The curriculum framework for AP Chinese includes six themes: 1) families and communities; 2) personal and public identities; 3) beauty and esthetics; 4) science and technology; 5) contemporary life; and 6) global challenges. These units overlap with one another in content and concept. No one theme is independent of any others. The new volumes echo the thematic framework of the AP curriculum, while acknowledging and embracing the themes' interconnected nature.

In the now volumes, units are grouped by theme, and each unit considers that theme's main content and contexts. All six themes embrace rich language and culture in a variety of authentic contexts. Each theme is organized into two to ten units (for a total of twenty-eight units). The structure closely aligns with the curriculum framework of AP Chinese, mainly in the intermediate range, but sporadically extending to advanced-low proficiency level. The units provide a preliminary collection of tasks within a thematic approach and are by no means an exhaustive list of topics to cover in AP Chinese, or in courses prior to and after AP Chinese. Each unit falls within a range of one to three sublevels, to allow teachers to customize the tasks to the level of proficiency in their classrooms.

The twenty-eight units are classified into three categories based on the scope and depth of the content knowledge in the unit, meaning how much that unit requires a teacher to spend extra time for self-study before getting ready to teach. The three categories are characterized as low-content, mid-content, and high-content. Low-content units do not require teachers to learn new content in different disciplines, whereas high-content units require teachers to reserve relatively extensive time to prepare a topic before teaching. Be kindly reminded that these classifications are not divided by exact or absolute cut-off boundaries, but instead give a sense of where each unit falls along a continuum of increasing scope and depth of content knowledge.

The following provides a list of units classified as low-content, mid-content, and high-content, according to the order presented in the new volumes.

Low-Content Units (12)
Gratefulness and filial piety
Growing up and happiness
Dating for you and me
Tell the story of an advertisement
Bring happiness home
Designing advertisements and posters
Advertisements in the East and the West
Educational tours and study abroad
Life at Chinese and American high schools
Having a hotpot

Parenting
School education

Mid-Content Units (13)
Filial piety in a new era
One-child policy
Chopsticks and family
Gender equality
My room and Chinese Feng Shui
Cyberbullying
Smartphone's influence on teenagers
Internet and life
Chinese food
Gift-giving culture
Healthy diet
Earth needs you and me
Environmental pollution and protection

High-Content Units (3)
Chinese historical courtyard homes (Siheyuan)
Health planner
Animal protection

As you plan your courses around the tasks in this book, some preparation is necessary, especially if you are new to task-based teaching. It takes time and an active, open mind to shift perspectives. We offer the following advice to facilitate your course-planning process.

1. Reserve enough time to go through all units in the volumes and create the course planner.
2. Get acquainted with the content and acquire knowledge in different disciplines as necessary.
3. Cover all six themes in the course, and select at least one or two units that represent each theme. Often, teachers choose to cover more units centered on contemporary life, as these tasks relate more directly to learners' life experience.
4. Include a balanced mixture of low-, mid-, and high-content units.
5. Begin teaching low-content units and move toward high-content units.
6. Select units that are as diversified and inclusive as possible.

7. Plan, modify, and enrich selected units to customize them for the learners in your classroom.
8. Conduct a needs analysis to be sure your course design will meet the diversified needs of learners in your classes before finalizing the units you will cover.
9. Constantly keep in mind what students can do, and raise the bar with reasonable expectations.
10. Adjust the selected units as the course proceeds, in frequent consultation with learners.

II. Cope with Adaptability and Flexibility

A task-based curriculum is like a chameleon: it is as adaptive and flexible as possible for the design and implementation of various tasks. As the teacher, you understand the many factors involved in the local dynamics of your classroom; be prepared to adjust accordingly and to consider the following.

1. Instructional Time

The units' proposed instructional time ranges in length from five to twenty hours. The estimated instructional times given here may not accurately project how much time investment is required for any one unit in all classrooms. As any task-based unit moves along, you will get a better sense of appropriate time management. Observe how students behave and grow in the learning process.

2. Sequential Tasks in One Unit

A unit with less instructional time is likely to have fewer tasks, while a unit with more instructional time tends to have more. It's up to you, the teacher, to decide which and how many tasks in a unit are critically needed for your class. Some units in the new volumes are long, and context is extensively explored. In some units, not all tasks can be fully implemented in class, given time constraints. When teaching a partial unit, using only a selection of tasks and skipping others, remember to fill in the missing content to ensure coherence in transitioning from one task or unit to another to ensure a modified, well-organized unit.

In each unit, tasks are sequenced developmentally from easy to difficult, from small scope to wider scope, from fundamental to higher levels of critical thinking skills, and from individual to societal, national, and international.

Many different types of tasks are included in the new volumes. They range in terms of structure, focus, centrality of linguistic features, authenticity, and type of interaction. Structure is used as a criterion to distinguish focused from unfocused tasks. Focused tasks have predetermined linguistic features, whereas unfocused tasks deal with them incidentally during the stage of task planning or when tasks are in action. Focused tasks are analogous to structure-orientated tasks, and unfocused tasks are analogous to communication-oriented tasks. The former relates more to pedagogical tasks, the latter to authentic tasks. Using type of interaction as a criterion, tasks include, but are not limited to: jigsaw, information gap, information exchange, problem solving, decision making, and opinion exchange. Tasks are fluid in type, and they allow and encourage creativity in design.

3. Authentic Materials and Authenticity

Authentic materials are intriguing, fun, motivating, and interesting. They are updated and current in content. If appropriately chosen, they can trigger curiosity and actively stimulate learners' five senses. Authentic materials means those that native speakers in Chinese-speaking communities see, read, listen to, write, and speak; they are not intentionally created for learners of Mandarin Chinese or any instructional purposes. Admittedly, as learners build up their competence, truly authentic materials may not yet be easily comprehensible. Semi-authentic materials therefore emerge to satisfy such a need. These are authentic materials that have been simplified in language use in order to suit the proficiency level of learners. The simplification process is necessary and inevitable before learners are competent enough to decode and interpret a diverse of authentic sources through a higher level of reading.

Authenticity is not necessarily achieved only through the use of authentic materials. A task that resembles the process of the negotiation of meaning among native speakers is also regarded as authentic. Asking students to communicate in a social context that connects with real-life experience conveys a high degree of authenticity. The tasks in the new volumes range in terms of degree and form of authenticity, vesting them with energy and vitality to reinvigorate a learner-centered setting.

4. Planning Time Outside of Class

Pre-planning of tasks saves in-class time and allows self-paced learning. If well-guided, this process helps learners improve in accuracy, fluency, and even complexity of language use. Designate some tasks that learners can complete at home and on their own, to encourage their autonomy and freedom. Self-learning opportunities also cater to individual differences in learning style, language proficiency, comfort zone, proximal learning, and open sources, to name a few. Pair or group work can be done outside of class to maximize peer interaction, aided by technology tools. While organizing tasks, plan for time for learners to do pre-tasks and post-tasks outside of class.

5. Step-by-Step Instructions

Each task includes step-by-step instructions, supplemented in some units by instructional strategies as reminders. Teachers can use the resources offered in full or partially; resources include, but are not limited to: handouts, tables, organizers, and different types of formative and summative assessments for interpretive, interpersonal, and presentational communicative tasks. They are ready to use in the classroom and can be easily modified for learners' needs. Imagine them as student worksheets or exercises, ready for teachers to copy and paste for immediate use.

6. Suggested Vocabulary and Structures

While it's possible to generate a comprehensive list of vocabulary and structures for beginning learners, it's harder to do so for students whose proficiency is intermediate to advanced-low. Although a list of language components is available in some units, these lists, when included, are not intended to be comprehensive. Incidental vocabulary, phrases, and structures may arise in the task-in-action process. We encourage you to be open-minded and pitch in whenever needed. Intermediate and pre-advanced learners should be well-equipped with self-regulated strategies in this aspect of learning. Encourage students to go out of their comfort zone and acquire new vocabulary, expressions, and structures. As their proficiency level increases, they will gain the independence, freedom, and autonomy characteristic of a self-learner in some sense. This is particularly true of learners with advanced-level proficiency. Take advantage of the highly accessible technology tools described in the new volumes (see section IV below) to assist independent learning.

7. Rubrics and Assessments

Not every task includes a rubric or checklist, but each unit includes at least one task-specific rubric. The rubrics and checklists can be conveniently revised if needed. In some sense, each task not only serves as an instructional component, but also fulfills the purpose of assessment. Instruction and assessment go hand in hand and support each other. Be mindful of whether instruction or assessment is the main focus, and plan each unit accordingly. More rubrics are created for speaking and writing presentational tasks, and fewer for interpretive and interpersonal tasks. Many interpretive tasks can be easily scored or graded due to the nature of the comprehension check items that are designed. Performance of interpersonal tasks is not always easy to assess precisely, especially when learners are conversing simultaneously in a highly interactive and noisy setting. But quick and ongoing observation, checking, and marking can be easily done for interpersonal communication.

III. Recycle and Spiral up to Maximize Learning Outcomes

Ideally, the intricacy of input-and-output learning process is integrated in the tasks themselves, but in reality, not every task can achieve this goal. How to best prepare students to work on one task and be confident in their transition to the next cannot be taken for granted. The keys to bridging the gaps between tasks are scaffolding, recycling, and spiral-ups. Although these are not explicit in some units in the new volumes, they are crucial to effective learning and smooth transitions during tasks and when moving from one to the next. These nuances of effective transitions determine the success of task implementation in cultivating high-performance learners.

To fill the gaps between tasks, teacher-led discussions, comprehension checks and formative assessments, and remedial instruction need to be done. Many teachers hold the misconception that teacher-led discussion should not be encouraged and is not as needed when using student-centered tasks. On the contrary, teacher-led or teacher-fronted scaffolding serves as a foundation for learners, equipping them with language functions they need for the next task. What matters is how to make these parts of the class meaningful and communicative.

When teacher-led discussion is taking place, comprehension checks take place simultaneously. Formative assessments can be added in whatever form is appropriate. This brings about remedial instruction to consolidate learning. Ideally the design of tasks themselves inherently fills the gap. When they do not, teachers need to do "here-and-now", teaching live and on the spot.

An excellent example of how to fill the gap mentioned above can be found in the unit Dating for You and Me. In this unit, the language components are inherently spiraled up and recycled in well-sequenced and connected tasks. This exemplifies an ideal design of tasks: not only does this sequence motivate students but it also effectively consolidates language learning through a genuinely engaging process.

The series of tasks in this unit begins with speed-dating task in three rounds of interviews between a boy and a girl. Then each girl and boy creates an imaginary future self, who then also participates in online dating. To complete this "future self" task online, each learner views approximately ten love profiles and chooses one as their dream friend of the opposite sex. This recycles language functions similar to the first "speed-dating" task, allowing learners to revisit target language use at the lexical, syntactical, and semantic levels. The third task in the sequence, face-to-face dating, requires more engagement and resembles what happens in the real world. The face-to-face dating task proceeds in two rounds: first, a girl dates a boy, and then a boy dates a girl. Interpersonal communication mingles with alternating presentational communication, constantly integrating learned language components in actions. To conclude the task cycle, students write an essay summarizing their dating experience.

While the sequence of three integrated, progressive tasks reinforces linguistic elements and achieves short-terms goals, an even more important spiral-up lies in an extension of the task sequence at the end of the semester to fulfill a long-term goal. About one month after the completion of the task cycle, students engage in peer learning by reading selected essays and answering comprehension check questions. Although this particular unit on dating might be more suited for college students than high schoolers, the principles of task design that recycle, integrate, and consolidate language functions can be readily adopted and modified for learners in secondary school settings in different contexts. Putting aside content and age-appropriate factors, the unit demonstrates well how the design of tasks carefully spirals up learned materials, saving teachers the work of creating something on their own to fill the gaps between tasks.

Interestingly, although the dating unit described above was rated as one of the top two units in terms of difficulty, students enjoyed it the most and rated it as the top favorable task during the semester when it was implemented. This proves that interesting and motivating tasks can ignite learners to be willing to take on challenges and do well.

IV. Empower Task-Based Learning with Technology

Technologies change rapidly. Digital authenticity harnesses the power of new technologies in task-based classrooms. Nowadays, a wide array of technology tools and applications, such as hyperlinked webs, multimodal social media, and app-rich mobile media, have transformed the learning of language and culture to be more active, engaging, and rewarding.

Tasks aided by technological tools have been found to be more effective than traditional teaching methods. The use of technology increases the interaction between teachers and students, enhances productivity of learning outcomes, and helps generate needed information instantly. To incorporate technology, instructors must implement the right technological tools to make the environment innovative for students. One useful strategy for choosing the correct technology tools is backward design. Curriculum design and objectives always govern the choice of technologies, not vice versa. Technology helps serve and fulfill instructional goals and objectives and can never outweigh curriculum and pedagogy.

Chapter 8 in this book highlights optimal blends of tasks and recent technologies to activate technology-mediated task-based learning at little or no cost. The chapter discusses strategic ways to achieve these optimal blends and pinpoints key benefits to integrating tasks in three communicative modes to achieve goals. It provides an introduction to the technology tools mentioned most frequently in the book, and gives advice on how to leverage the affordances of accessible technologies in nontrivial, creative ways that closely align with task-based instructional objectives. The tools include Baidu instant translation tool, Polleverywhere, Nearpod, Google Form, EdPuzzle, Flipgrid, Padlet, Voice Thread, and Quizlet, among others. Although the book offers only a glimpse of the many tools available in educational fields, the ones we highlight are very user-friendly and have gained prominence and popularity in language learning in recent years. Specifically, they are used to create communicative tasks, enhance interactions, and assess language performance in three communicative modes. In Chapter 8, brief descriptions and virtual tours through screenshots, images, and photos will help you get some ideas and think more deeply about how these tools can be related to the achievement of pedagogical goals.

High-performing teachers can help their students to progress three times as fast as students with low-performing teachers. The new volumes prepare teachers to be high-performing in a task-based classroom, and ultimately to cultivate students to be high-performing task learners.

Please note the following precautions for technology use.
1. Consider pedagogical purposes first, and technology second.
2. Technology can theoretically facilitate learning, but not because of the technology itself. Always put curricular and pedagogical goals upfront.
3. Use the technology tool that you feel more comfortable and familiar with instead of spending time exploring something that is too time-consuming.
4. Avoid using fancy technologies that don't contribute to your instructional and pedagogical objectives.
5. Consult with learners on their preferences of technology tools and applications.
6. Whenever a certain technology tool or application is included or recommended in a unit, refer to the introduction of that particular tool and application in Chapter 8.
7. Finally, technology itself isn't that important. It's how you use it that matters.

Chapter 2

Families and Communities　家庭与社区

Unit 1: Filial Piety in New Era　孝顺的时代意义

Contributors: Hui Chen, Huichee Yeh, James Jones
Proficiency Level: Intermediate-High
Instructional Time: 8-10 hours
Can-Do Statements:
1. Students can comprehend, interpret, and discuss the concept of 孝顺 from a video clip and the results of an online survey.
2. Students can identify actions that are considered as 孝顺 in Chinese culture and share their reflections and perspectives about 孝顺.
3. Students can generate their own definition of 孝顺 and compare 孝顺 standards in Chinese culture and their own cultures.
4. Students can interview Chinese native speakers about 孝顺 and present their findings to their peers in both written and oral formats.

Task 1　A Story of a Family　"家"的故事

Communicative Mode: Interpretive and Interpersonal

Step 1: Watch the following video clip about the concept of 孝顺 in Chinese culture. 请看一个中国文化里关于"孝顺"的小电影：
https://youtu.be/cDOAgF6atAk

Step 2: Discuss the following questions with your classmates. 和你的同学讨论下面的问题：

1. 这个小电影有几个不同的时间点？在这些时间点里发生了什么事？
2. 这个家有几口人？他们的关系是什么？
3. 这家人为什么会吵架、起冲突？
4. 电影里的小男孩为什么对他爸爸说："爸，奶奶这样对你和妈，你还为她难过？"
5. 爸爸给奶奶唱了一首歌，请你猜一猜，他唱的歌是什么意思？
6. 电影最后有这样两句话："上一代的榜样"和"下一代的模范"。你认为这两句话是什么意思？

7. 电影最后，我们看到了一个很大的"家"字。你认为这个小电影以"家"字作为结尾，是想告诉观众什么？
8. 看完电影，你认为什么是"孝顺"？"孝"与"顺"分别代表什么意义？

Suggested Key Words and Structures:

孝顺	xiàoshun	filial piety
榜样	bǎngyàng	example, model
模范	mófàn	model
尊重父母	zūnzhòng fùmǔ	respecting parents
孝敬老人	xiàojìng lǎorén	respecting and pay filial piety to parents and the elderly
结婚	jiéhūn	to marry
婚姻	hūnyīn	marriage
孝子	xiàozǐ	sons who pay filial piety to parents
孝女	xiàonǚ	daughters who pay filial piety to parents
不孝	búxiào	not paying filial piety to parents
孝心	xiàoxīn	the best wish for paying filial piety to parents
三代同堂	sāndàitóngtáng	three generations living together in one house

Task 2　The "24孝" Standards　"24孝"标准

Communicative Mode: Interpretive, Interpersonal, and Presentational

Step 1: Read the following chart of the 2012 revised version of "24孝" standards in China.
读一读 2012 年中国的 "24孝" 标准：

新 "24孝" 行动标准

1、经常带着爱人、子女回家
2、节假日尽量与父母共度
3、为父母举办生日宴会
4、亲自给父母做饭
5、每周给父母打个电话
6、父母的零花钱不能少
7、为父母建立"关爱卡"
8、仔细聆听父母的往事
9、教父母学会上网
10、经常为父母拍照
11、对父母的爱要说出口
12、打开父母的心结
13、支持父母的业余爱好
14、支持单身父母再婚
15、定期带父母体检
16、为父母购买合适的保险

17、常跟父母沟通　　　　　21、和父母一起锻炼身体
18、带父母一起出席重要的活动　22、适当参与父母的活动
19、带父母参观你工作的地方　　23、陪父母拜访他们的老朋友
20、带父母去旅行或故地重游　　24、陪父母看一场老电影

Step 2: Complete the "Google survey" about your perceptions of the 2012 revised "24孝" standards in China. 完成谷歌问卷调查，填写你对中国新"24孝"标准的看法。

Google Survey/Handout Questions

新"24孝"标准	你做到了吗？	你觉得合理吗？	是你以后努力的目标吗？
1. 经常在家跟父母在一起			
2. 节假日尽量与父母共度			
3. 为父母举办生日宴会			
4. 亲自给父母做饭			
5. 每周给父母打个电话			
6. 不向父母要太多零花钱			
7. 为父母建立"关爱卡"			
8. 仔细聆听父母的往事			
9. 教父母学会上网			
10. 经常为父母拍照			
11. 对父母的爱要说出口			
12. 打开父母的心结			
13. 支持父母的业余爱好			
14. 支持单身父母再婚			
15. 定期陪父母体检			
16. 为父母推荐合适的保险			
17. 常跟父母沟通			
18. 带父母一起出席重要的活动			

（续表）

19. 带父母参观你的学校和常去的地方			
20. 陪父母去旅行或故地重游			
21. 和父母一起锻炼身体			
22. 适当参与父母的活动			
23. 陪父母拜访他们的老朋友			
24. 陪父母看一场老电影			

Instructional Strategies:

An alternative to the Google form is to create a hard copy for the students to write down their answers. The teacher may consider removing the following 6 items and simply include the rest 18 items in the survey for discussion. Please note that some of the standards are only applicable to adults, such as the 1st, 6th, 15th, 16th, 19th, and 20th. They could be slightly revised to fit a teenager's life experience:

1. 经常带着爱人、子女回家→经常在家跟父母在一起
6. 父母的零花钱不能少→不向父母要太多零花钱
15. 定期带父母体检→定期陪父母体检
16. 为父母买合适的保险→为父母推荐合适的保险
19. 带父母参观你工作的地方→带父母参观你的学校和常去的地方
20. 带父母去旅行或故地重游→陪父母去旅行或故地重游

Step 3: After finishing the survey, complete the following self-checklist by categorizing the items from the survey (their numbers) and elaborate your reasons. 做完问卷以后，填写下面的总结表格，并说明你的理由。

思考问题	新"24孝"号码	理由
我做到了		
我没做到		
合理		
不合理		
未来努力的目标		

Step 4: Exchange and compare the results of your self-checklist of "24孝" with your peers. 和你的同学交换问卷，看看你们写得一样吗？

Instructional Strategies:
The teacher can release the automatically generated statistical charts and tables to the entire class. If the survey is completed by hand, then the tally of the statistics can be done in class as a group.

Step 5: Discuss the following questions based on the results of the self-checklist completed by you and your peers. 根据你和同学的问卷结果，讨论下面的问题：

1. 中国的新"24孝"标准你都做到了吗？你是怎么做的？
2. 根据中国新"24孝"标准，你觉得你孝顺吗？为什么？
3. 根据美国或者你自己文化的标准，你觉得哪些新"24孝"标准是合理的？哪些是不合理的？为什么？请根据你自己的想法，用几个句子写下"孝"的定义。
4. 在新"24孝"标准中，你最想做到哪些？为什么？请选出至少5个标准。你可以根据自己的想法做一些修改。

Instructional Strategies:
The teacher may lead the whole class to discuss the results of the first 6 questions in the following three aspects: 1）你做到了吗？ 2）你认为合理吗？ 3）这是你未来努力的目标吗？ This process sets an example of what you expect students to do in the follow-up group discussions. Let the students work in groups to discuss and analyze questions 7-24, and most importantly, provide possible interpretation for each question. Each group would get 4-6 questions depending on the size of the class.

Step 6: Share what you have discussed with the class. 和全班同学分享你的小组讨论的内容。

Instructional Strategies:
Ask each group to present their analysis and interpretation. While one group is presenting, other students should take notes and engage in class discussions. Teacher can also lead the class to generate a summary of the results of the survey and apply what students can do to treat their parents better.

Suggested Key Words and Structures:

显示	xiǎnshì	to show, to reveal
参与	cānyù	to participate
调查问卷	diàocháwènjuàn	survey
选择／选	xuǎnzé/xuǎn	to choose
其中	qízhōng	among

百分比 / 比例	bǎifēnbǐ/bǐlì	percentage
全部	quánbù	all
大部分 / 大多数	dàbùfèn/dàduōshù	majority
少部分 / 少数	shǎobùfèn/shǎoshù	minority

Task 3 Is Achieving "24孝" Easy? 做到"24孝"容易吗？

Communicative Mode: Interpretive, Interpersonal, and Presentational

Step 1: Read the following news report that summarizes an online survey of the "24孝" standards completed by native speakers of Mandarin Chinese in China. 读一读下面关于中国人对新"24孝"看法调查的新闻。

http://cq.cqnews.net/html/node_175208.htm

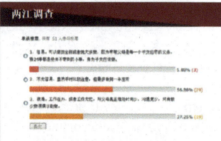

Step 2: After reading the article, answer the following questions. Then discuss your responses with your partner and analyze the content of the article. 读完新闻，请回答下面的问题。然后和你的同学讨论并分析新闻的内容。

1. 这篇文章的标题是"近7成网友认为做好新'24孝'不容易"，"近"与"7成"是什么意思？
2. 这份调查的目的是什么？
3. 这份调查是面对面访问，还是在网上进行的？
4. 一共有多少人参与了调查？
5. 多少网友认为新"24孝"容易做到？为什么？
6. 多少网友认为新"24孝"很难做到？为什么？

Step 3: Compare the results of the class survey with those in the above article in 3 aspects: 1) factual description, 2) possible interpretation, and 3) conclusion. 从三个方面对比课上同学们的调查问卷结果和这则新闻的结果：1）事实的描述；2）调查结果出现的原因；3）总结。

Step 4: Use the following template to write a simulated online report that analyzes and summarizes the results of the class survey and upload it to a class Google Drive. 用下面的模板写一个课堂调查问卷报告，上传到谷歌网盘。

Template for writing a survey report:
Part 1 (Introduction): Time adverbial (month, date, specific point of time), an organization/school/unit ＋ 对 ＋ survey topic ＋ 进行了（一份）调查，一共……参与调查．
Part 2 (Body): 其中，analysis of percentage for each item (factual information at the descriptive level), explanation and interpretation.
Part 3 (Conclusion): 调查显示……，summary.

Step 5: Read your classmates' report on the Google Drive. Comment on at least 3 journal entries with 1-3 sentences for each. 读一读你的同学写的报告，给三位同学写评论，每个评论写1到3句话。

Suggested Key Words and Structures:

An organization/place ＋ 对 ＋ topic of a survey ＋ 进行了调查	(An organization/place) ...... conducted a survey on a topic ......
The number of respondents ＋ 参与了调查	(The number of respondents) ...... participated in the survey
人 ＋ 表示 ＋ opinions or stance	Someone expressed that ...... (opinions or stance)

调查数据＋显示＋the result of a survey	Data of the survey shows that ...... (result of the survey)
网友	netizen
……占很大的比例	...... has high percentage on
将近／大约	almost/around
绝大多数	overwhelming majority
应尽的义务	obligation
苛刻	rigor
相处	get along with
沟通	to communicate
偶尔	occasionally

Comparison and contrastive devices:

比较 (verb) A 与 B＝拿 A 与 B 做一个比较	to compare A with B
在……方面	in the aspect of ......
在我看来；对我而言；对我来说	in my opinion; from my perspectives
相比之下，……	comparatively speaking, ...
反过来说，……	on the contrary, ...
A 和 B 有很大的不同（差异）／相似点（相同点）	A and B has major difference/similarity

Organizational devices:

第一，第二，第三，最后	first, second, third, lastly
首先，其次／再则，除此之外，最后	first, second, in addition, lastly
总而言之	in short; in conclusion

Rubric for Summary of and Comments on an In-Class Survey on "24 孝"

Criteria	4	3	2	1
Organization	Completely adheres to the 3-part template	Adheres to the 3-part template	Partially adheres to the 3-part template	Little adherence to the 3-part template
Information	Rich and comprehensive	Sufficient	Some	Little

(Continued)

Criteria	4	3	2	1
Language	A variety of vocabulary and structures appropriately used	Vocabulary and structures appropriately used	Some vocabulary and structures inappropriately used	Little vocabulary and limited structures; pervasive errors
Peer Interaction	3 or more comments with excellent quality	3 comments with good quality	2 comments with acceptable quality	0-1 comments; dissatisfactory; quality

Task 4   An Interview   小采访

Communicative Mode: Interpersonal and Presentational

Instructional Strategies:
After creating a list of questions with the teacher's help, students are paired up to interview a native speaker of mandarin Chinese. The teacher will first need to call and choose suitable families in the local community. Consider the appropriateness of the students' age and have parents present during the interview. Suggest students record the interview with permission and listen to it again after the interview. If finding native speakers of Chinese is not feasible, students can work in pairs to discuss the questions below and write an essay based on the discussion.

Step 1: Interview a Chinese native speaker about his/her thoughts of 孝顺 with a partner. Please set up the interview time with the person and conduct the interview after school. Below are some of the questions you may use during the interview. If possible, record the interview and listen to it again. The interview can be done face-to-face or online. 和你的同学一起采访一个中文母语者，问问他/她对孝顺的看法。请你们和受访者约好时间在课后进行采访。采访的时候，你们可以问下面的问题。如果可以，请你们录音，采访之后再听一遍。你们可以面对面采访，也可以线上采访。

采访问题：
1. 你家有几口人？他们是谁？做什么工作？
2. 你的父母多大年纪了？他们还健在吗？他们住在哪儿？

3. 你觉得什么是"孝顺"？你在生活中是如何孝敬父母的？请你举一些例子。
4. "孝顺"是中国的传统美德，而美国人有这样的观念吗？在你看来，中美在这个问题上有哪些差异？
5. 你同意下面五个有关"孝顺"的陈述吗？为什么？
    1)"不孝有三，无后为大"，没有孩子就是不孝顺。
    2）为了符合父母的期待，选择父母要自己选的专业。
    3）父母老了以后，跟自己住在一起，而不去住养老院。
    4）为了让父母高兴，让父母决定自己的婚姻。
    5）其他你想问的问题。

Possible questions to start the interview:
采访者姓名：
受访者姓名：   性别：   年龄：   工作：
采访日期：   采访地点：

Your interview should follow this flow:
1. 感谢受访者
2. 自我介绍
3. 采访的目的
4. 开始采访
5. 结束采访

Step 2: Bring your responses and notes to the class and share and discuss with other pairs. 请你把你采访的记录带到课堂上，和同学一起讨论。

Instructional Strategies:
This "think, pair, share" process helps students practice and build their confidence. Students first discuss in pairs, and when they are ready and feel comfortable, they can speak in front of the entire class.

Step 3: Following your teacher's lead, report and discuss with the whole class about your findings and compare differences between Chinese culture and your own culture. 在老师的带领下，和全班一起讨论你的采访结果，对比一下中国文化和你自己的文化中对"孝顺"的看法。

Rubric for Writing Presentational and Speaking Interpersonal

A. Task completion (10 pts.)
Timely submission of the typed interview notes (2 pts.)
   YES   NO
Timely submission of summary report (2 pts.)
   YES   NO
Participation/contribution to in-class discussion (6 pts.)
   Excellent   Good   Acceptable   Unacceptable

B. Elaboration of thoughts and perspectives (30 pts.)
Comprehensive notes taken during interview, supporting thoughts and evidence, idea progression, organization, and coherence
   Excellent (25-30 pts.)   Good (20-24 pts.)
   Acceptable (15-19 pts.)   Unacceptable (0-14 pts.)

C. Language delivery (50 pts.)
Evidence of connective, comparative, contrastive, and organizational language elements at the sentence/paragraph levels
   Excellent (46-50 pts.)   Good (41-45 pts.)
   Acceptable (31-39 pts.)   Unacceptable (0-30 pts.)

D. Length (10 pts.)
   Excellent: 500 Chinese characters or more (10 pts.)
   Good: 400-499 Chinese characters (8-9 pts.)
   Acceptable: 300-399 Chinese characters (4-7 pts.)
   Unacceptable: fewer than 300 Chinese characters (0-3 pts.)

Chapter 2

Families and Communities　家庭与社区

Unit 2: Gratefulness and Filial Piety　感恩与孝顺

Contributor: Lee-Mei Chen
Proficiency Level: Intermediate-Mid to Intermediate-High
Instructional Time: 8 hours
Can-Do Statements:

1. Students can understand the videos about one's life path and parental love, discuss its meaning, and discuss their own experience related to their childhood and growth.
2. Students can create a thank-you card to express their appreciation to their parents.
3. Students can understand the film on love and filial piety and compare different aspects of cultural values and traditions in Chinese culture and the culture of their own.
4. Students can summarize their own film and present their perspectives and analysis of parental love in Chinese culture and cultures.

Task 1　Feeling Grateful　感恩的心

Communicative Mode: Interpretive, Interpersonal, and Presentational

Step 1: Watch the following video clip. 请看下面的电影短片。
https://www.youtube.com/watch?v=a5SYMboaZ6A

Step 2: Discuss the meaning of the video with your partner. 和你的同学讨论这个电影短片的意义。

Step 3: Watch the video again, then fill in the form below according to the content. 再看一遍电影短片，根据电影内容填写下面的表格。

一岁时	
三岁时	
五岁时	
十一岁时	
十四岁时	
十六岁时	
十八岁时	
二十岁时	
二十四岁时	
二十七岁时	
二十九岁时	
三十三岁时	
结语	
你的补充或想说的话	

Step 4: Watch another video, starting from 0:48. 请看另一个电影短片，从 48 秒开始看。

https://www.youtube.com/watch?v=NHruW8cOyZ0

Step 5: After watching, discuss what you have seen with your classmates. 看完上面的电影短片，请和你的同学一起讨论你看到了什么。

Step 6: Watch the video again, and fill in the blanks below according to the video. Then discuss the answers with the whole class. 再看一遍电影短片，根据电影内容填空。然后和你的同学讨论你们的答案。

1. 当我很小的时候……
   当你还很小的时候，他们花了很多时间，（1）教你用 _____ 吃东西；（2）教你 _____，_____，_____，_____，_____，_____，_____；教你（3）_____ 的道理。
   你是否还记得（1）你们 _____ 了很久，才学会的第一首 _____；（2）经常 _____ 他们，你是 _____ 来的。

2. 所以，当父母变老的时候……
   所以，当他们有天变老时，
   当他们（1）_____不起来，或（2）_____不上话时，
   当他们（3）_____ _____一些老掉牙的（4）_____，请不要（5）_____
   他们。
   当他们开始（1）_____、_____；（2）_____、梳头时，手开始不
   停地（3）_____；请不要（4）_____他们。
   因为你在慢慢长大，而他们（1）_____在慢慢（2）_____。只要你在他们
   （3）_____的时候，他们的心就会很（4）_____。

3. 如果有一天……
   如果有一天，当他们站也（1）_____，走也（2）_____的时候；请你紧紧
   （3）_____他们的手，（4）_____他们慢慢地走。就像当年他们（5）_____
   你一样。
   极其（1）_____却又（2）_____的感情，（3）_____在他们和我的心里，
   （4）_____我们走过一生。

   "树欲（1）_____而（2）_____不（3）_____，子欲（4）_____而
   （5）_____不（6）_____。"

Step 7: Discuss the following questions and share ideas with the class. 讨论下面的问题，并和全班同学分享你的看法。

1. 小时候父母帮你做了什么事？想一想父母在食、衣、住、行、娱乐各方面给你们的帮助。
2. 想一想，当你的父母慢慢变老的时候，你愿意帮他们做什么？会跟电影里描述的一样吗？
3. 请解释"树欲静而风不止，子欲养而亲不待"这句话的意义，以及它给你的启示。这句话传达的概念与美国人的看法有什么不同？（欲→要，待→等待）
4. 什么是父母对子女的爱？中国父母对子女的爱与美国父母对子女的爱有什么不同？

Instructional Strategies:
这是皋鱼说给孔子的话，主要在宣扬儒家的孝道。是从反面来说明行孝要及时，要趁着父母健在的时候，而不要等到父母去世了才想要尽孝。

Step 8: Design a thank-you card, write 5-10 sentences to express your appreciation to what your parents have done for you. 设计一张感谢卡，在卡片上写5到10句你向父母表达感谢的话。

Rubric for the Thank-You Card

Content
4 Rich information and well-connected thoughts
3 Good amount of information with connected thoughts
2 Limited information with some ideas
1 Lack of information

Language Use
4 Idiomatic expressions and appropriate use of different structures
3 Appropriate use of words, expressions, and some structures
2 Some inappropriate use of words, expressions, and structures
1 Many inappropriate use of words and structures

Creativity & Design
4 Graphics and language well-matched; full of creativity and attraction
3 Graphics and language matched; with a certain level of creativity and attraction
2 Graphics and language somewhat mismatched; mediocre originality and attraction
1 Graphics and language mostly not matched; lack of creativity and attraction

Task 2   *The Farewell*   《别告诉她》

Communicative Mode: Interpersonal and Presentational

Step 1: Watch the movie *The Farewell* (Billi's family returns to China under the guise of a fake wedding to stealthily say goodbye to their beloved grandma — the only person that doesn't know she only has a few weeks to live). 看电影《别告诉她》（比莉一家回到中国，假装参加婚礼，实际上是和不知道自己病重的奶奶道别）。

(Note: The instructor should purchase the DVD or online streaming for this movie first.)

Step 2: In class, work in pairs to complete the following table based on the plot of the movie. Then discuss your answers with the class. 根据电影情节和你的同学在课上填写下面的表格。然后和全班同学一起讨论。

这是哪一种类型的电影？	☐ 喜剧	☐ 悲剧	☐ 悲喜剧
电影里谁得了癌症？	☐ 奶奶	☐ 爸爸	☐ 结婚的表哥

得癌症的人，知道自己得了癌症吗？	☐ 知道	☐ 不知道	☐ 看不出来
电影里面大家一起吃饭时，是用什么样的桌子？	☐ 圆桌	☐ 长桌	☐ 不一定
电影里一开始比莉坚持说实情，后来呢？	☐ 仍坚持	☐ 不管了	☐ 不坚持了
在病人面前，每个人都能表现得好像没事一样吗？	☐ 可以	☐ 不行	☐ 两种都有
在中国电影里，很多重要的事都是在饭桌上表现出来的，为什么？	☐ 饭好吃就愉快	☐ 吃饭就不会反对	☐ 家人吃饭团聚好商量
在中国传统里，一个人的成就是谁的功劳？	☐ 父母的	☐ 自己的	☐ 朋友的
在中国传统里，一个人的生命是属于谁的？	☐ 家庭的	☐ 自己的	☐ 孙子的

Step 3: In a group of 3 to 4, discuss the following questions, then each group takes turns to report to the class. 三到四位同学一组，讨论下面的问题。然后每组轮流在全班报告。

1. 对于家人不告诉病人真正的病情，你怎么看？
2. 对于医生不告诉病人真正的病情，你怎么看？
3. 医院让病人的家人更改病情报告给病人看，你有什么看法？
4. 你认为应该让病人本人知道她的真正病情吗？
5. 你希望你的爷爷（或奶奶）每天健身、跟你通电话吗？
6. 你喜欢这部电影吗？为什么？
7. 在这部电影里，你最喜欢哪个角色？为什么？
8. 在这部电影里，你认为谁演得最好？为什么？
9. 你认为这部电影最大的特点是什么？
10. 一般东方人都尊重长辈，把自己的成就说成是长辈父母的功劳，你同意吗？为什么？
11. 如果你是奶奶，你希望知道实情吗？为什么？
12. 如果你是比莉，你会怎么做？为什么？
13. 根据报道，很多人看了这部电影都哭了，你觉得是为什么？

14. 在电影院里，你看到华裔还是非华裔观众比较多？ (optional)
15. 在电影院里，你看到都是什么样年龄层的观众？ (optional)

Step 4: Work in pairs to complete the following table about cultural values and traditions in China and the U.S., then elaborate your perspectives. 和你的同学一起完成下面关于中美文化价值和传统的表格，然后详细说明你的看法。

	中国	美国
知道亲人得癌症，心里会难过	☐	☐
会让病人自己知道他得了癌症	☐	☐
找机会让所有的亲人回来告别	☐	☐
亲人跟病重的人相处，表现都像平常一样	☐	☐
很在乎结婚的场面及面子问题	☐	☐
自己有病或有事常常不告诉家人，自己来解决	☐	☐
好好对待身边的亲人，随时问候	☐	☐
注重一家人的亲情	☐	☐
医生也跟家人合作不告诉病人真正的病情	☐	☐

Step 5: The whole class will be divided into two groups. One group expresses thought in favor of telling the patient the truth, and the other speaks in favor of not telling the truth. Then discuss and compare ideas of the two groups. 全班同学分为两组，一组同学说明告诉奶奶真相的理由，另一组同学说明不告诉奶奶真相的理由。然后两组同学讨论、比较双方的看法。

Instructional Strategies:
Teachers can use a Venn Diagram to summarize the reasons for both groups and lead the students to discuss and compare their thoughts.

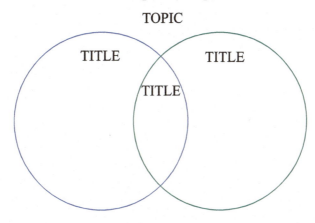

Step 6: In a group of 3 to 4, discuss the following questions pertaining to the possible generation gaps, cultural values and customs. Then discuss and exchange ideas with the whole class. 三到四位同学一组，讨论两代人可能会出现的代沟、价值观和文化传统。然后和全班分享交流。

1. 你会用父母教育你的方式去教育下一代吗？
2. 你和你父母那一代，对于"爱"的表达方式有什么不同？
3. "妈妈，对不起！"和这部电影各在传达什么主题？
4. 你长大后离开家，你将如何照顾你的父母？
5. 你长大后离开家，如果你得了癌症，你会如实告诉父母吗？
6. 你认为"三代同堂"或和父母一起住，有什么优缺点？你会选择哪一种？
7. 你长大后，当父母有病痛时你会如何对待他们？
8. 你会如实告诉父母他们的真正病因吗？为什么？
9. 当你年老生病时，你会希望你的孩子如实告诉你真正病因吗？为什么？
10. 古人说："报喜不报忧"，你现在自己有病痛都没告诉父母；以后你的孩子离家读书，对你也是报喜不报忧，你怎么看？

Extended questions:
1. 常听中国老一辈的人说，子女的成就都是父母的功劳，而不提自己，你怎么看？
2. 这部电影里有一个旅馆的服务生，跟女主角比莉谈婚姻，谈美国的事，问一些个人的事情，也给了她很多个人意见。这样的情况跟个人隐私有关吗？谈谈你对个人隐私的看法。
3. 有些中国人真的管太多了，跟你第一次见面，却问了一堆问题，也给你一堆的建议。你怎么回应，才不会失礼？

4. 中国的父母或亲戚常常过分关心子女与异性交往的情况与他们的婚姻状况，也就是会有催婚的情形。你对这种现象有什么看法呢？
5. 你希望你未来的先生或太太是什么样的人？
6. 你做事喜欢自己一个人做决定，还是喜欢跟别人讨论以后再做决定？
7. 你希望你未来的另一半，跟你学一样的专业还是有不同的专业？为什么？

Step 7: Use the guided questions above to organize your thoughts and write an essay by incorporating the structures listed in Task 2. Feel free to go out of your comfort zone to self-acquire words and expressions. 用上面的讨论问题作为指导，写一篇文章（请使用这个任务后面列出的句型）。你也可以使用自己查到的词汇和短语。

Instructional Strategies:

The focus and scope of the essay relevant to the film can be further determined by the instructor. It is recommended that the essay contain the following information:

Required information for the essay:

1. Brief description of the film
2. Comments on actors and actresses
3. Cultural values, traditions, and customs in Chinese culture
4. Cultural values, traditions, and customs in my own culture
5. Compare and contrast two cultures
6. Conclusion

Suggested Key Words and Structures:

我觉得……既……又……	I think ...... is not only ......, but also ......
……不但……，而且……	...... not only ......, but also ......
……在表达……	...... is expressing ......
……尽管……可是……	although ...... but ......
先……，然后……，最后……	First ......, then ......, at last ......
……是……中最……的	...... is the most ...... of ......
……常常会反映出……	...... often reflects ......
在中国/美国的社会里/文化中，……	In Chinese/American society/culture, ...

Rubric for Essay

	4	3	2	1
Organization	Well-organized and coherent with ideas progressively, well presented	Organized and coherent with ideas being appropriately developed	Ideas and thoughts indicative of incompleteness and somewhat incoherent	Ideas and thoughts lack of coherence and development
Vocabulary and Phrases	The essay uses vivid words and phrases. The choice and placement of words seems accurate, natural, and not forced.	The essay uses vivid words and phrases. The choice and placement of words is inaccurate at times and/or seems overdone.	The essay uses words that communicate clearly, but the writing lacks variety.	The essay uses a limited vocabulary. Jargon or clichés may be present and detract from the meaning.
Structures, Grammar, and Mechanics	All 8 key structures included. Sentences well-constructed. No or minimal errors in grammar and mechanics.	At least 7 key structures included. Most sentences well-constructed. Several errors in grammar and mechanics, minimal interference with comprehension.	4-6 key structures included. Most sentences well-constructed. Some errors in grammar and mechanics that interfere with some understanding.	1-3 key structures included. Sentences awkward, distractingly repetitive, or difficult to understand. Numerous errors in grammar and mechanics that interfere with understanding.
Elaboration	Thoughts are fully articulated.	Thoughts are somewhat addressed.	Thoughts are incompletely addressed or unaddressed.	Lack of thoughts and ideas.

Chapter 2

Families and Communities　家庭与社区

Unit 3: One-Child Policy　独生子女政策

Contributor: Luoyi Cai
Proficiency Level: Intermediate-High to Advanced-Low
Instructional Hours: 6-8 hours
Can-Do Statements:

1. Students can understand and describe the development of China's population policies as well as its impacts upon China's society.
2. Students can exchange their opinions with Chinese native speakers on China's population policies, i.e. one child policy which has been changed to two-child policy currently, from their own perspectives.

Task 1　A Survey　小调查

Communicative Mode: Interpretive and Interpersonal

Step 1: Complete a survey through Poll Everywhere . 请用 Poll Everywhere 完成一个小调查。

Instructional Strategies:

The instructor presents the survey report and asks students to share the reasons for their answers to the last question：说说你为什么希望／不希望自己是独生子女？

Title
你的爸爸妈妈有几个孩子?

Title
你是家里的第几个孩子?

Title
你希望自己是独生子女吗?

Text, image URL, or LaTeX
希望

Text, image URL, or LaTeX
不希望

Step 2: Recently, the Chinese government changed its policy, allowing all families to have two children. Imagine how Chinese kids might react to the potentiality of having a sibling? Let's watch a video clip of a group of Chinese kids born after 2010 being asked "你要弟弟妹妹吗？", think about the following questions while watching it and discuss with your classmates. 最近，中国政府改变了人口政策：所有的中国家庭都可以生两个孩子了。想象一下，如果问中国的小孩子"你要弟弟妹妹吗？"，他们会怎么回答？看一个视频，一群2010年以后出生的中国小朋友对爸爸妈妈要第二个孩子有什么看法？请你一边看，一边想一想下面的问题，然后和你小组里的同学讨论。

https://www.youtube.com/watch?v=YGU79koScbs&list=FLtS5G9jFe8aDXjDUTJLfSvw

1. 哪个孩子的回答让你印象最深刻？为什么？
2. 视频里的中国父母对生两个孩子有什么忧虑？他们担心什么？

Step 3: Discuss the following question and post your opinions on the bulletin boards below. 和你的同学讨论下面的问题，把你的看法贴在相应的版块上。

在你看来，做独生子女的好处多还是坏处多？有什么好处？有什么坏处？

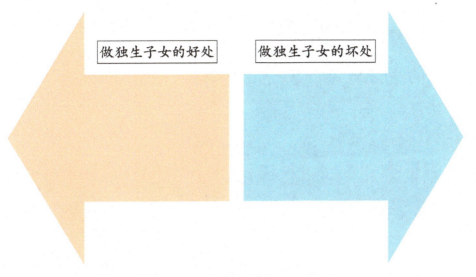

Task 2　Change of Slogans and One-Child Policy
　　　　从计划生育标语看政策变迁

Communicative Mode: Interpretive, Interpersonal and Presentational

Step 1: Use Quizlet to preview topic-related vocabularies before class. 在课前通过 Quizlet 预习相关生词。

Step 2: The following pictures of birth-control slogans and posters were taken in different historical stages, reflecting the propaganda of Chinese government for its birth-control policies. Read the picture captions and figure out the meanings of the slogans. Create an English caption on the picture. Then post your bilingual picture captions together with the pictures on Padlet. 下面的图片是中国不同历史时期独生子女政策的标语。读一读图解，想一想标语是什么意思。请你根据理解写一个英文版的标语。把中英文标语和图片都放在 Padlet 上做图文展示。

Instructional Strategies:
The instructor may divide the class into four groups and assign each group two pictures.

Group 1

图1 "该流不流扒房牵牛"
1980年中国政府正式开始提倡"一对夫妇只生育一个孩子"。1982年计划生育成为中国的基本国策。早期的标语内容往往冷漠强硬，缺乏人文关怀。图1是1997年，中国中部农村的一个计划生育标语："该流不流扒房牵牛"。"流"指超过生育指标必须做"人工流产"。

图2 "严禁生育超计划的二胎和多胎"
1990年，福建泉州街头挂着的计划生育标语：严禁生育超计划的二胎和多胎。

Group 2

图3 "计生条例已修订；超生罚款可不轻；超生一胎一万四；二胎两万五千整"
2003年，河南农村计划生育宣传标语。

图4 "农村计划生育家庭奖励制度"

2004年开始,全国部分农村开始实施计划生育家庭奖励制度。图4为2005年11月28日,苏北农村6名60岁以上的农民领取全年奖励金人民币600元。

Group 3

图5 "生男生女都一样,女儿更孝爹和娘"

记者调查发现,中国很多农村地区普遍存在重男轻女的现象。如果一个家庭没有儿子,会被很多人看不起。于是,没有儿子的家庭要么想办法去抱养一个男孩,要么男主人在外面找一个小老婆生孩子。

图6 "举报并协助查实利用B超非法鉴定胎儿性别的,奖励现金20000元"

计划生育还加剧了人口的性别失衡,因为生儿子是一个传统偏好,很多家庭利用选择性堕胎的方式来确保生一个儿子。在一些地区,想生儿子的父母会把已经出生的女婴卖出去。一位中国学者表示,当时80%的弃婴是女孩。

Group 4

图7 "地球妈妈太累了，再也撑不起太多孩子"
2007年，国家开始计划生育标语的"洗脸工程"，清理冷漠标语口号，使用新的"更人性"的标语。

图8 "小康，紧张，恐慌"
独生子女政策在2008年左右变得宽松了很多。这个政策的支持者认为：独生子女政策为中国减少了约4亿人口，让中国的孩子获得更好的资源，也提高了大多数中国家庭的生活水平。

（以上图片、文字改编自：http://guoqing.china.com.cn/2013-11/22/content_30678124_17.htm）

Suggested Key Words and Structures:

标语	biāoyǔ	slogan
提倡	tíchàng	advocate
计划生育	jìhuà shēngyù	birth control
国策 = 国家政策	guócè = guójiā zhèngcè	national policy
人工流产 = 堕胎	réngōng liúchǎn = duòtāi	abortion
指标	zhǐbiāo	index
严禁	yánjìn	strictly forbid
一胎	yītāi	one-child; only child
超生	chāoshēng	have more children than the family planning policy stipulated

超过	chāoguò	exceed
罚款	fákuǎn	fine; penalty
奖励	jiǎnglì	incentive; reward
制度	zhìdù	system; regulation
重男轻女	zhòngnán qīngnǚ	preference of boys to girls
抱养	bàoyǎng	adopt (a child)
加剧	jiājù	aggravate
性别失衡	xìngbié shīhéng	gender imbalance
确保	quèbǎo	insure
弃婴	qìyīng	abandoned infants
冷漠	lěngmò	unconcerned; indifferent
强硬	qiángyìng	tough
人性	rénxìng	humane
恐慌	kǒnghuāng	panic
支持	zhīchí	support
资源	zīyuán	resource

Step 2: Each group prepares a 5 minutes' presentation about the assigned posters, including a Q&A session. The presentation should include the following information. 每组准备一个五分钟左右的报告，包括一个问答环节。报告须包括以下内容：

1. 介绍一下你在照片上看到了什么？照片上的标语是什么意思？
2. 这些标语可能出现在什么时候、什么地方，反映了什么社会问题？

Instructional Strategies:

After the presentation, the instructor may require one of three groups presenting to ask a question based on their presentation. Each student should ask at least one question throughout the presentations.

Rubric for Presentation

Categories	4	3	2	1
Organization and Content	Presentation is very well organized with well-connected discourse and minor errors	Presentation is well organized with appropriate discourse with occasional errors	Presentation is loosely organized with some inappropriate discourse with frequent errors	Presentation is poorly organized, with many errors that obscure meaning
Language Use and Functions	Rich and appropriate vocabulary, with wide range of sentence structures	Appropriate vocabulary, with some different sentence structures	Mostly appropriate vocabulary, with a few different sentence structures	Limited appropriate vocabulary, with frequent errors, mostly simple sentence structures
Delivery and Communication	Natural pace and intonation, with minimal hesitation or repetition	Smooth pace and intonation, with occasional hesitation or repetition	Generally consistent pace and intonation, with some hesitation or repetition	Inconsistent pace and intonation, with often hesitation and repetition
Tones and Pronunciation	Tones and pronunciations are always accurate, can be understood without difficulties by native speakers who are not used to speaking to second language learners	Tones and pronunciations are generally accurate, can be understood most of the time by native speakers who are not used to speaking to second language learners	Tones and pronunciation are sometimes not accurate, native speakers who are not used to speaking to second language learners have difficulties from time to time to understand the content due to the inaccuracy of tones and pronunciations	Tones and pronunciation are mostly inaccurate, even native speakers who are used to speaking to second language learners have difficulties to understand the content due to the inaccuracy of tones and pronunciations
Question & Answer	Understand the presentation well and the question given is kept to the point and insightful	Understand the presentation well and the question given is kept to the point and basically clear	Understand most of the presentation and the question given is basically related to the presentation	Barely understand the presentation and the question given is irrelevant and unclear

Task 3 A Story of an Adopted Chinese Girl
一个被领养的中国女孩的故事

Communicative Mode: Interpretive and Interpersonal

Step 1: Scan-read the following introduction story and watch a BBC news video about a Chinese girl adopted by an American couple going back to China to meet her biological parents. 先快速阅读下面的故事简介，然后观看一则有关"一个被领养的中国女孩"的新闻视频。

凯蒂（Kati，中文名：徐静芝）生下来的第三天，就被爸爸妈妈遗弃了（yíqì; abandon）。当时是1994年，中国正在实施（shíshī; implement）独生子女政策。

她的父母徐礼达和钱粉香当时已经有了一个女儿徐晓晨，由于担心无法抚养（fǔyǎng; raise）和受到惩罚（chéngfá; penalty），他们偷偷把徐静芝放在街头。

一年后，一对美国夫妇肯（Ken）和茹思（Ruth）从孤儿院（gū'éryuàn; orphanage）领养（lǐngyǎng; adopt）了她，并把她带回美国密歇根州。但凯蒂的婴儿包（yīng'ér bāo; swaddling cloth）中有一个亲生父母（biological parents）留下的字条（zìtiáo; message）。因为这个字条，她在20年后回到杭州，在断桥上与亲生父母相会。

视频链接：https://www.bbc.com/zhongwen/simp/media-42312887

Step 2: In three groups, discuss the following questions from three different perspectives. Group 1 discusses from Kati's perspective; Group 2 discusses from the biological parents' perspective; Group 3 discusses from the American adoptive parents' perspective. 大家分成三组，从凯蒂、凯蒂的亲生父母、凯蒂的美国养父母三个视角讨论相关问题并与大家分享你们的观点。

Group 1 Discussion questions:
1. 如果你是凯蒂（Kati），你会选择回中国找你的亲生父母吗？为什么？
2. 你能理解亲生父母为什么遗弃你吗？你会不会原谅（yuánliàng; fogive）他们？为什么？

Group 2 Discussion questions:
1. 如果你是凯蒂（Kati）的亲生父母，你会决定跟凯蒂见面吗？为什么？
2. 看到她以后，你想对她说什么？

Group 3 Discussion questions:
1. 如果你是凯蒂（Kati）的美国父母，你会不会告诉女儿关于亲生父母的事？你会怎么告诉她？
2. 你愿意支持凯蒂回中国找她的亲生父母吗？为什么？

Task 4 From "1" to "2": Change of China's One-Child Policy
从"1"到"2"：中国独生子女政策的改变

Communicative Mode: Interpretive and Interpersonal

Step 1: Use Quizlet to preview some relevant vocabularies and do online research on the following key words about China's population policies. 在课前通过 Quizlet 预习相关生词，并上网查询、了解一些有关中国人口政策的关键词。

Suggested Key Words and Structures:

经济	jīngjì	economy
实施	shíshī	implement
政策	zhèngcè	policy
严格	yángé	strict
赡养	shànyǎng	to support; to provide for (senior family members)
尽孝	jìnxiào	to fulfill filial duty
增长	zēngzhǎng	growth; increase
减速	jiǎnsù	decelerate
加速	jiāsù	accelerate
老龄化	lǎolínghuà	population aging
放宽	fàngkuān	loosen (policy/requirement......)
放开	fàngkāi	release
生育	shēngyù	fertility
高峰	gāofēng	peak
成本	chéngběn	cost

Step 2: Do some research online on the following terms, share the information you have found in the comments sections under the respective terms. 请上网找一找有关下面几个词的资料，把你找到的资料通过回复贴到相应的 Padlet 标签下。

- 独生子女政策：
- 单独二胎：
- 全面二孩／二胎：

Step 3: Watch the following video twice: A video introducing China's population control policies. After watching the video, use Nearpod to complete the chart below. 请观看一段有关中国计划生育政策的视频，一共看两遍。看完视频后，根据视频中的内容填写下面的思维导图。

Instructional Strategies:
The instructor could pause at the important information parts.
https://www.bbc.com/zhongwen/simp/multimedia/2015/11/151102_video_explainer_one_child_policy

传统的中国家庭是什么样的？

• "多子多福"是什么意思：

_____年，中国开始实施独生子女政策；于是，中国出现了很多"4+2+1"家庭，就是：

• 为什么要实施独生子女政策？

1980年开始，独生子女政策发生了什么变化？
2013年：
如今：

• 为什么改变独生子女政策

Step 4: Take a look at Chart 1 and think about the following question. 看看图表1，想一想下面的问题。

- 2016年中国政府全面开放二胎以来，中国的新增人口有没有增加？

Chart 1

Step 5: Take a look at Chart 2 and think about the follow-up question. 看看图表2，想一想下面的问题。

- 为什么中国政府开放二孩政策以后，中国的新增人口并没有增加？

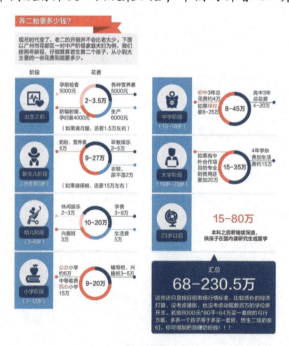

Chart 2

Step 6: Discuss in groups, use the same pattern of Chart 2 to make a chart, listing the cost of raising a child in the U.S. 根据图2，和你的同学讨论并制作一张"美国育儿成本"的图表，列出以下信息：

- 在美国养一个孩子，从出生前到开始独立工作需要多少钱？花费在哪些方面？

Task 5　Mini-Documentary　微纪录片

Communicative Mode: Interpersonal and Presentational

Step 1: Work in groups of 3-4 students. Each student interviews one Chinese friend about his/her own experience of growing up in an one-child or non-one-child family, as well as his/her opinions on China's one-child policies. Film the interviews and merge the group members' interviews into a mini-documentary with a maximum length of 15 minutes. Groups share the mini-documentaries the next class, and after playing the mini-documentaries, give a 2 minutes reflection on your documentaries and answer any questions from other groups. 3-4个学生为一组，每组每位同学采访一位来自中国的朋友（每位组员选取的采访对象不可为同一个人），了解中国朋友在独生子女／非独生子女家庭中的成长经历以及他们对中国计划生育政策的看法。将各个采访过程摄制下来，每组剪辑出一个不超过15分钟的微型纪录片。学生们在下一节课中以小组为单位，展示每一组的微型纪录片；每组的微型纪录片播放后，该组成员对他们的纪录片作一个2分钟的心得分享，并回答其他小组成员的提问。

Rubric for Mini-Documentary Project

Categories	4	3	2	1
Organization and Content	The mini-documentary is very rich in content with insightful questions and sufficient details, well-organized with minor errors	The mini-documentary is rich in content with clear questions and some details, well-organized with occasional errors	The mini-documentary has basically clear questions, but lack of details; loosely organized with frequent errors	The mini-documentary is poorly organized, with many errors that obscure meaning
Language use and Functions	Rich and appropriate vocabulary, with wide range of sentence structures	Appropriate vocabulary, with some different sentence structures	Mostly appropriate vocabulary, with a few different sentence structures	Limited appropriate vocabulary, with frequent errors, mostly simple sentence structures
Delivery and Communication	The interview is conducted in natural pace and clear question delivery, with minimal hesitation or repetition	The interview is conducted in smooth pace and intonation, with occasional hesitation or repetition	The interview is conducted in generally consistent pace and intonation, with some hesitation or repetition	The interview is conducted in inconsistent pace and intonation, with often hesitation and repetition
Tones and Pronunciation	Tones and pronunciations are always accurate, can be understood without difficulties by native speakers who are not used to speaking to second language learners	Tones and pronunciations are generally accurate, can be understood most of the time by native speakers who are not used to speaking to second language learners	Tones and pronunciation are sometimes not accurate, native speakers who are not used to speaking to second language learners have difficulties from time to time to understand the content due to the inaccuracy of tones and pronunciations	Tones and pronunciation are mostly inaccurate, even native speakers who are used to speaking to second language learners have difficulties to understand the content due to the inaccuracy of tones and pronunciations
Reflection and Q&A	The reflection is well-organized with clear logic; full of insightful ideas. Understand audience's questions well and the answer given is kept to the point.	The reflection is basically in clear logic and the opinions are basically well-connected. Understand audience's questions and the answer given is basically clear.	The reflection has some opinions, but are loosely organized. Have some difficulty in understanding audience's questions and the answer given is unclear though still relevant.	The reflection barely has understandable opinions; poorly organized. Don't understand the audience's questions and the answer given is irrelevant.

Chapter 2

Families and Communities 家庭与社区

Unit 4: Chopsticks and Family 筷子与家庭

Contributor: Lee-Mei Chen
Proficiency Level: Intermediate-High to Advanced-Low
Instructional Time: 8-10 hours
Can-Do Statements:

1. Students can understand the content of a video, demonstrate how to use chopsticks appropriately, and teach others how to use them.
2. Students can understand a passage on chopsticks, identify taboos, traditions, and cultural perspectives, and compare the similarities and differences in using chopsticks in China, Japan, and South Korea.
3. Students can understand and interpret the content of a video, recognize the significance of chopsticks that relates to Chinese family values, and appreciate the different traditions of using chopsticks in Chinese culture.
4. Students can exchange information and interview native Chinese speakers to deepen their understanding of the traditions of using chopsticks in Chinese culture.
5. Students can give an oral presentation and perform a skit on cultural traditions of using chopsticks.

Task 1   How to Use Chopsticks Correctly?   如何正确使用筷子？

Communicative Mode: Interpretive

Step 1: Watch the video till the end. Discuss the following questions. 看完下面的视频，和同学讨论问题。

https://www.youtube.com/watch?v=DljaMs-KLOc

1. 这个视频教你们什么？你们看到了什么？
2. 谁用过筷子？你会用筷子吗？
3. 你在哪儿用过筷子？在什么地方用过筷子？
4. 谁知道怎么用筷子？请说一说你用筷子的经验。
5. 用筷子的时候，要用到手的哪些部位？
6. 怎么说五个手指头的名字？还有怎么说第一个手指头跟第二个手指头中间的地方？

47

Step 2: The teacher introduces the vocabulary (i.e. finger names and the space between the thumb and the index finger) needed to describe how to use chopsticks. 学习手指和手掌部位的名字：拇指、食指、中指、无名指、小指、虎口。

Instructional Strategies:
Use the Total Physical Response (TPR) strategy to demonstrate and guide students to follow the instructions correctly.

Step 3: Watch the video again part by part, then practice how to use chopstick with your partner. 分部分看视频，然后和你的同学练习筷子的用法。

第一部分：0:16-0:26
视频的说明：将第一根筷子用虎口夹紧并放在无名指之上
老师的说明：
1）把五个指头打开
2）再把小指跟无名指弯起来
3）然后把第一根筷子放在虎口跟无名指上面
4）在虎口这个地方把筷子夹紧

第二部分：0:26-0:38
视频的说明：将第二根筷子置于中指之上，利用拇指与食指将其固定
老师的说明：
1）把第二根筷子放在中指上，也就是中指跟食指中间
2）然后用拇指跟食指把第二根筷子夹好

第三部分：0:38-0:57
视频的说明：运用食指及中指移动筷子，进行夹取动作，运用拇指当支点，食指及中指移动筷子，下面筷子固定不动
老师的说明：
1）拇指不动，中指不动，下面的筷子也不动
2）好，现在食指上下动一动，再动一动
3）对了，现在你们知道怎么用筷子夹中国菜了

Instructional Strategies:
1. The video uses formal language at the advanced level to explain how to use chopsticks. Linguistically, this is beyond students' comprehension level. However, the video is still a good choice as the 3-step demonstration provides clear and vivid visual aids and clues that are key to learning. Guide students to pay attention to the demos

instead of the language use: Pause the video after each designated segment, as indicated above, and demonstrate each step in sequence. After demonstrating each step, ask students to show and explain how to use chopsticks in groups, in pairs, and/or then individually. Repeat the same procedures for three times.

2. The use of formal language in the video has been converted to comprehensible input at the intermediate level and above. The repetitive use of the 把字句 in meaningful and authentic contexts will make the learning process much easier. Please note that teaching vocabulary isolated from contexts is by no means as effective as the procedure above.

3. To help students generate expected language output, always start from recognition activities, i.e., students receiving input from the teacher and acting it out, and then move to production activities, i.e., students acting it out and explaining verbally.

Step 4: Ask students to show and explain how to use chopsticks in groups, in pairs, and/or then individually. 先分组，然后单独介绍并演示筷子的用法。

Step 5: Practice using chopsticks to pick up popcorn and see who can get the most out of the bowl in a timed competition activity "谁最会用筷子？" using popcorn and M&M chocolates your teacher supplies. Then, switch from popcorn to M&M chocolates. 玩游戏"谁最会用筷子？"看谁能最快把爆米花和M&M从一个杯子夹到另一个杯子！

Instructional Strategies:
The teacher brings popcorn and M&M chocolates to class and put them in paper bowls or cups.

Task 2　The Chopsticks Culture　筷子文化

Communicative Mode: Interpretive, Interpersonal, and Presentational

Step 1: Read the passage. 读一读下面的这篇文章。
https://m.sohu.com/n/477625517/

Instructional Strategies:
1. The teacher cuts the article into three parts — 中国的筷子文化、日本的筷子文化、韩国的筷子文化. Explain the article by using three examples of chopsticks. Illustrate the phrases below in the three parts:

厚重、文化深厚、刀叉、围坐在圆桌、烹煮、油炒的菜比较油滑、够着离自己远的盘子、用餐过程、摆放、长短不一、木质筷子、寓意、"敲碗敲筷子，讨吃一辈子"、贫穷、浓厚的亲情、混用、天圆地方、世界观、海产品、剔除鱼刺、日本料理、繁文缛节、不祥的征兆、定食、卫生筷、捧碗、端起饭碗、热火朝天、亲情四溢、小碟子、撕开泡菜

2. The teacher should bring three kinds of chopsticks to class (bamboo, wood, iron or stainless steel, etc. — Chinese style, Japanese style, Korean style), and let the students hold each of them. Students can also talk about their experiences using them and vote on which one they prefer to use.

3. To fully engage students in active listening and discussion, ask students to take down notes and prepare questions while reading the articles and listening to presentations in class.

Step 2: Read 中国的筷子文化 again with your partner. Discuss the following questions. 再读一遍"中国的筷子文化"，和你的朋友讨论下面的问题。

1. 中国人喜欢围坐在什么样的桌子，用什么餐具来吃饭？
2. 中国菜大多是油炒的，用什么样的筷子会比较方便？
3. 中国人使用筷子有什么禁忌？
4. 说说中国人对于筷子什么样的情形下，会有"死亡"、"贫穷"的意思。
5. 中国筷子的形状有什么世界观？为什么？

Step 3: Read 日本的筷子文化 again with your partner. Discuss the following questions. 再读一遍"日本的筷子文化"，和你的朋友讨论下面的问题。

1. 为什么日本的筷子头比较尖一点？
2. 为什么日本的筷子都是比较短的，而且多用木筷子？
3. 日本人使用筷子有什么禁忌？
4. 为什么日本人每个人都有自己的用餐"专筷"？
5. 什么是"卫生筷"？

Step 4: Read 韩国的筷子文化 again with your partner. Discuss the following questions. 再读一遍"韩国的筷子文化"，和你的朋友讨论下面的问题。

1. 为什么韩国的筷子都是以铁制的为主？
2. 为了能比较方便地剥开鱼刺、撕开泡菜，韩国的筷子大都是什么形状的？
3. 在韩国，"捧碗吃饭"代表什么意思？
4. 韩国人吃饭，什么时候不用筷子？
5. 韩国家庭吃饭时，哪一点与中国人很像？

Step 5: Work with a partner to compare the cultural traditions of chopsticks among the three countries. Fill in key phrases in the table below. 和你的同学一起，对比不同国家的筷子文化，填写下面的表格。

	长短样式	使用方式	筷子的材质	代表的意义	使用时的禁忌	有什么共同点
中国						
日本						
韩国						

Step 6: Read the three parts of the article again and then ask your Chinese friends about the questions below. 再读一遍上面的文章，问你的中国朋友下面的问题。

1. 吃饭的时候，对于拿起筷子有什么样的规矩及禁忌？
2. 吃饭的时候，一定要端起饭碗吗？为什么？
3. 小孩可以比大人先拿起筷子夹食物吗？
4. 以前的人认为，拿筷子的上下位置对于孩子的未来，有什么样的传说？
5. 自己的筷子可以和别人的筷子碰撞吗？为什么？
6. 一般来说，在美国长大的孩子平时吃东西使用刀叉的机会比筷子多，你会坚持你的下一代要学会使用筷子吗？为什么？
7. 你对于我使用筷子的方式，有什么建议？
8. 你认为东方人使用筷子与西方人使用刀叉，各有什么优点？
9. 在日本家庭里，每个人都有自己的专用筷子。你会坚持在自己家里每个人各自使用自己的筷子来吃饭吗？为什么？
10. 你去外面吃饭，会自己准备筷子吗？为什么？
11. 现在在外面吃中国菜时，每盘菜都有公筷母匙，你觉得好吗？为什么？

Step 7: Share your findings in your own group and give a presentation to the whole class. You may use the following sample patterns. 和你的同学说一说你采访中国朋友的结果。你可以用下面的示范句子。

Suggested Sentence Patterns:
- 通过我的访问，我了解到一般中国人吃饭的时候……
- 关于怎么拿筷子和碗，………
- 老一辈的中国人认为筷子拿得高一点或低一点，……
- 吃饭的时候，自己的筷子和别人的筷子……

- 在美国的中国家庭,吃饭的时候还是习惯用筷子,因为……
- 至于筷子的使用/在筷子的使用方面,我(不)希望我的孩子将来……
- 我……时候开始学用筷子,目前……
- 我认为筷子和刀叉……
- 在日本人家里,每个人都有自己的专用筷子,我的看法是……
- 中国人吃饭,常会帮别人夹菜,现在盘子上都有公筷母匙,我觉得……
- 为了……,我在外面吃饭的时候,……筷子……
- 在生活上,我觉得中国人使用的筷子……

Rubric for Oral Speech

	4	3	2	1
Thoughts and Coherence	Thoughts are elaborate and well-developed, substantially organized and coherent.	Thoughts are adequately developed, generally organized and coherent.	Thoughts are slightly appropriate but somewhat disconnected and undeveloped.	Thoughts are predominantly undeveloped.
Language Competence	Excellent grasp of structures and vocabulary	Good grasp of structures and vocabulary with occasional errors	Using structures and vocabulary with some consistent errors	Incompetent with frequent errors
Fluency and Pronunciation	Continuous speech with little stumbling, intelligible pronunciation	Generally smooth speech, sporadic pauses, mostly intelligible pronunciation	Slow speech with pauses and hesitations	Halting and uneven speech
Speech's Deportment	Good eye contact with the audience without looking at a paper	Some eye contact with some of the audience, without looking at a paper	Little to no eye contact with the audience; awkward and unnatural bearing and gestures	Entire speech is read off of a paper; visibly uncomfortable and/or fidgeting

Task 3   Different Meanings of the Chopsticks   筷子代表的各种意义

Communicative Mode: Interpretive, Interpersonal, and Presentational

Step 1: Watch the video below. 看一遍下面的视频。

https://www.youtube.com/watch?v=Af8P8M9aXxA

Step 2: Watch the video again and pause at 0:24. Discuss the questions below. 看视频，在24秒处停下，讨论下面的问题。

1. 这个爷爷用筷子给孙子吃什么？
2. 孙子尝了一次以后，为什么还想再尝？
3. 银幕上写出"启迪"这两个字，是什么意思？

Step 3: Continue to watch the video and pause at 1:06. Discuss the questions below. 看视频，在1分06秒处停下，讨论下面的问题。

1. 那天的晚餐叫什么？
2. 那个小女孩为什么在哭？
3. 谁教她使用筷子？
4. 银幕上写出"传承"这两个字，是什么意思？

Step 4: Continue to watch the video and pause at 1:33. Discuss the questions below. 看视频，在1分33秒处停下，讨论下面的问题。

1. 那群人聚在一起在吃什么饭？
2. 小男孩伸出筷子夹菜被阻止，大人说了什么？
3. 银幕上写出"明礼"这两个字是什么意思？

Step 5: Continue to watch the video and pause at 2:05. Discuss the questions below. 看视频，在2分05秒处停下，讨论下面的问题。

1. 那个年轻人几年没有回去看他的母亲了？
2. 他的母亲做什么给他吃？
3. 银幕上写出"关爱"这两个字，是什么意思？

Step 6: Continue to watch the video and pause at 2:32. Discuss the questions below. 看视频，在2分32秒处停下，讨论下面的问题。

1. 那位先生在父母的牌位前摆上筷子和碗，说了什么？
2. 银幕上写出"思念"这两个字，是什么意思？

Step 7: Continue to watch the video and pause at 3:15. Discuss the questions below. 看视频，在 3 分 15 秒处停下，讨论下面的问题。

1. 中国人认为过年过节一个人吃年夜饭，合适吗？
2. 请人来家里一起吃饭，说"多双筷子嘛！"是什么意思？
3. 银幕上写出"睦邻"这两个字，是什么意思？

Step 8: Continue to watch the video and pause at 3:58. Discuss the questions below. 看视频，在 3 分 58 秒处停下，讨论下面的问题。

1. 那位先生送给他的太太什么东西？说了什么？
2. 那个礼物是给谁用的？
3. 银幕上写出"守望"这两个字，是什么意思？

Step 9: Continue to watch the video and pause at 4:32. Discuss the questions below. 看视频，在 4 分 32 秒处停下，讨论下面的问题。

1. 年夜饭桌上，每摆一双筷子代表什么？
2. 那个小男孩说了哪些成语？各代表什么意思？
3. 银幕上写出"感恩"这两个字，是什么意思？

Step 10: Divide the class into eight groups, each group chooses one focal topic from the following eight topics: 启迪、传承、明礼、关爱、思念、睦邻、守望、感恩, to create a skit on chopsticks and perform it in front of the class. 全班同学分成八组，每组选一个小标题：启迪、传承、明礼、关爱、思念、睦邻、守望、感恩，向全班做口头报告。

Guided questions:
1. 什么样的情形是"启迪"？如何用筷子为主角来表达出"启迪"？
2. 什么样的情形是"传承"？如何用筷子为主角来表达出"传承"？
3. 什么样的情形是"明礼"？如何用筷子为主角来表达出"明礼"？
4. 什么样的情形是"关爱"？如何用筷子为主角来表达出"关爱"？
5. 什么样的情形是"思念"？如何用筷子为主角来表达出"思念"？
6. 什么样的情形是"睦邻"？如何用筷子为主角来表达出"睦邻"？
7. 什么样的情形是"守望"？如何用筷子为主角来表达出"守望"？
8. 什么样的情形是"感恩"？如何用筷子为主角来表达出"感恩"？

Self-checklist:
1. Does your group's performance connect to chopsticks?
2. Does your performance relate to the focal topic that your group has chosen?

3. Does your performance include at least 5 expressions or structures listed below?
4. Is the content of performance well organized?
5. Does your performance last for at least 4 minutes?

Suggested Key Words and Structures:

启迪	qǐdí	enlightenment
明礼	míng lǐ	know when to be polite
关爱	guān'ài	care
睦邻	mùlín	get along with your neighbors
守望	shǒuwàng	keeping the vitality of the future

尽管……，还是 / 仍然……
除了……以外，还有……
……就……了
开始的时候……，可是现在……
有一点儿……
一点儿也不……
不但……而且……
太……了
先……再……然后……最后……

Rubric for the Oral Skit (Same score for members in the same group)

Grading Criteria	4	3	2	1
Organization and Content	An extraordinary quantity and quality of understanding the topics, no typos	A quantity and quality of somewhat understanding the topics, very few typos	The information of the topics is included, but somewhat disorganized and some typos	The information of the topics is missing or disorganized, many typos
Language Use and Functions	Mastery of formulaic expressions, vocabulary and structures	Familiar with formulaic expressions, vocabulary and structures	Inconsistent use of formulaic expressions, vocabulary and structures	No mastery of formulaic expressions, vocabulary and structures
Delivery and Communication	Excellent performance; communication with ease; very fluent and smooth skit; pronunciation similar to a native speaker's pronunciation; everyone in the group gets chance for delivery	Good performance, making some pauses in the delivery; no or little interference with communication; somewhat fluent and clear skit; satisfactory pronunciation; everyone in the group gets a chance for delivery	The performance has several pauses and awkward moments; having a few problems in communication; several problems with fluency, and halting skit; several syllables or words are mispronounced; not everyone delivers the performance	The performance seems very uncomfortable; frequent communication breakdowns; halting skit; many words and syllables are mispronounced; only one or two members in the group do the delivery

Chapter 3

Personal and Public Identities 个人和社群认同

Unit 1: Growing up and Happiness 成长与快乐

Contributor: Lee-Mei Chen
Proficiency Level: Intermediate-Low to Intermediate-Mid
Instructional Time: 6-8 hours
Can-Do Statements:

1. Students can understand and recite a classic Chinese poem.
2. Students can interpret the videos on a happy childhood and growth, discuss the importance of parenthood in relation to their growth, and identify the ideals of the parent's role.
3. Students can discover the joy and value of growing up, respecting the elderly, and caring for the world.
4. Students can describe their future work and lifestyle, and future husband/wife.

Task 1   Classic Poems 古诗

Communicative Mode: Interpretive and Interpersonal

Step 1: Read the following poem. 读一读下面的古诗。

回乡偶书
「唐」贺知章
少小离家老大回，乡音无改鬓毛衰。
儿童相见不相识，笑问客从何处来。

Instructional Strategies:
Teacher can follow these steps to help students better understand the poem.

1. Students circle the characters that they are able to recognize.
2. Teacher guides students to discuss the characters that they are able to recognize.
3. Teacher guides students to discuss the characters that are new to them.
4. Teacher elicits responses from students to explain the meaning of each sentence and what the poet tries to express.

回乡	huíxiāng	回到家乡
偶书	ǒushū	随便写写的诗
老大	lǎodà	老，脸上变老；大，年龄变大
乡音	xiāngyīn	家乡的口音
无改	wú gǎi	没什么变化
鬓毛衰	bìnmáo cuī	鬓毛，脸上额角边靠近耳朵的头发；衰，老年人毛发变少了
相见	xiāngjiàn	看见我
不相识	bù xiāngshí	不认识
笑问	xiào wèn	笑着问
从何处来	cóng héchù lái	从哪里来的

Chinese translation:
我在年少的时侯离开家乡，到了老年才回来。我说话的家乡口音虽然没有改变，但鬓角的毛发却已经变白变少了。家乡的小孩看到我都不认识我。还笑着问：客人，您是从哪里来的？

Step 2: Based on the classic poem and the modern Chinese translation, tell the story about this poem. 根据原诗和翻译，用现代汉语讲一个故事。

Step 3: In pairs, (1) recite the poem; (2) discuss what kind of feeling this poem expresses; (3) talk about what you want to be when you grow up, and why. 两个人一组，先背诵这首诗，然后讨论这首诗表达了什么意思，最后说一说你长大以后想做什么，为什么。

Instructional Strategies:
The teacher may explain the theme of the poem after the discussion. 教师分析本诗主旨：这两句诗，通过变与不变的对比，表达出诗人对人容易变老、世事也会改变的感叹，也表达出诗人对家乡的深深感情。

Task 2　Growing up Happily　快乐地成长

Communicative Mode: Interpretive and Interpersonal

Step 1: Watch this music video twice, then fill in the blanks. 看这首歌曲的视频，然后填空。

https://www.youtube.com/watch?v=An5HR-ZQBOo

快乐成长

看，我们的 _____ 多 _____，
看，我们的 _____ 多 _____，
听，我们的 _____ 多 _____，
听，我们的 _____，
用 _____ 感受师长的 _____，
_____ 所有的 _____，
双手虽小，_____ 远大，
我们就是国家社会未来的 _____，
懂得 _____，努力 _____，快乐 _____。

Step 2: Watch the following video, then discuss the questions below in class. 看视频，然后和同学讨论下面的问题。

https://www.youtube.com/watch?v=Rf8vOS_Clpg

1. 为什么孩子的每个活动，父亲都缺席？
2. 在影片中为什么用一台提款机来代替父亲？
3. 这部影片在告诉我们什么？

Step 3: Work with your partner to discuss and fill in the blanks below. 和你的同学讨论并填写下面的表格。

理想中的父母	赞成	不赞成
孩子的活动都能参与		
每个月给零用钱		
叮嘱、协助我做功课		
每天叫我起床		
做饭给我吃		
不要处处管我		
让我自由选择课外活动		
不要限制我上网的时间		
有困难时能找他们商量		
需要时能随时在身边		

Step 4: Share your results with the whole class and report on the characteristics of an ideal parent. 跟全班讨论你们的填表结果，说一说理想的父母是什么样的。

Task 3 Growing up and the Future 成长与未来

Communicative Mode: Interpretive, Interpersonal, and Presentational

Step 1: Watch the short video and discuss the following questions. 看视频，讨论下面的问题。

https://www.youtube.com/watch?v=NwgwGCzukKo

1. 这个女孩的爸爸去哪里了？
2. 为什么最后女孩说，爸爸我可以哭了吗？
3. 你认为这部影片在告诉我们什么？

Step 2: Within 5 minutes, write down 3 sentences that describe one of the most memorable event that happened to you in the past, then share your sentences with the class. 请用 5 分钟时间写三句话，描述以前发生的印象最深的事，然后和全班分享。

Step 3: Within 5 minutes, write down 3 sentences that describe your current hobbies, then share your sentences with the class. 请用 5 分钟时间写三句话，描述你现在的爱好，然后和全班分享。

Step 4: Within 5 minutes, write down 3 sentences that describe your future career, then share your sentences with the class. 请用 5 分钟时间写三句话，描述你以后想从事的职业，然后和全班分享。

Suggested Connected Words:
记得 …… 曾经 …… 后来 ……，…… 比我想象的还要 ……，本来 …… 后来 ……
这是我 …… 虽然 …… 可是 ……

Step 5: Watch this video, then discuss the following questions. 看下面的视频，讨论下面的问题。
https://www.youtube.com/watch?v=2z_sc1PGdog

1. 这些人为什么在雨中蹦跳？
2. 他们的心情如何？
3. 你认为只有孩子才会在雨中快乐地蹦跳吗？
4. 看了这部影片，你会问你自己什么？
5. 如果你就站在旁边，你会加入这些人吗？
6. 请问你上次感到幸福，是什么时候？什么会让你感到幸福？

7. 你觉得什么样的人生是幸福的？
8. 你希望你今后的丈夫/妻子是什么样的？什么样的丈夫/妻子会让你觉得幸福？
9. 你以后想做什么工作？你想要什么样的生活方式？为什么？

Step 6: Discuss in pairs about what your future life and husband/wife would be like. 和你的同学说一说你希望你以后的丈夫/妻子是什么样的人？

Suggested Vocabulary:
长相清秀、英俊挺拔、高高瘦瘦、笑脸迎人、身体健壮、体贴入微、为人正直、看起来顺眼、戴眼镜、长头发、短发可爱型、很谈得来、爱看书的、爱逛街的、喜爱美食的、乖巧斯文、口若悬河、木讷寡言、活泼可爱的……

Step 7: Write an essay that includes the the following contents: (1) one of the most memorable event that happened to you in the past; (2) your current hobbies; (3) your future career. 请写一篇作文，说一说你印象最深的一件事，你现在喜欢做的事，还有你今后的职业和展望。

Suggested Key Words and Structures:
记得……，曾经……，后来……
……比我想象的还要……
本来……，后来……
这是我……，虽然……，可是……

Professions:

编辑	editor	厨师	chef
法官	judge	电影明星	movie star
歌星	singer	演员	actor
工程师	engineer	建筑师	architect
律师	lawyer	老师	teacher
校长	headmaster	摄影师	photographer
护士	nurse	记者	journalist
警察	police	教练	coach
科学家	scientist	电脑工程师	IT engineer
音乐家	musician	艺术家	artist
会计师	accountant	秘书	secretary
清洁工	janitor/custodian	图书馆员	librarian
研究员	researcher	运动员	athlete
总统	president		

Rubric for Essay

	4	3	2	1
Organization	Included opening, middle and ending; all the three requirements included	Included opening, middle and ending; two requirements included	Not clear on opening, middle and ending; two requirements included	No opening, middle and ending; only one requirement included
Vocabulary	The author uses vivid words and phrases. The choice and placement of words seems accurate, natural, and not forced.	The author uses vivid words and phrases. The choice and placement of words is inaccurate at times and/or seems overly done.	The author uses words that communicate clearly, but the writing lacks variety.	The writer uses a limited vocabulary. Jargon or clichés may be present and detract from the meaning.
Sentence, Structure, Grammar, Mechanics and Spelling	All sentences are well-constructed and have varied structure and length. The author makes no errors in grammar, mechanics, and /or spelling.	Most sentences are well-constructed and have varied structure and length. The author makes a few errors in grammar, mechanics, and/or spelling, but they do not interfere with understanding.	Most sentences are well-constructed, but they have a similar structure and/or length. The author makes several errors in grammar, mechanics, and/or spelling that interfere with understanding.	Sentences sound awkward, are distractingly repetitive, or are difficult to understand. The author makes numerous errors in grammar, mechanics, and/or spelling that interfere with understanding.
Elaboration	Thoughts are fully articulated and future career is thoroughly planned.	Thoughts are somewhat addressed and future career is roughly planned.	Thoughts are incompletely addressed or unaddressed and future career is slightly planned.	Lack of thoughts and ideas, no future career planned.

Chapter 3

Personal and Public Identities   个人与社群认同

Unit 2: Gender Equality   男女平等

Contributors: Miao-fen Tseng and Shuishui Long
Proficiency Level: Intermediate-High
Instructional Time: 10-12 hours
Can-Do Statements:

1. Students can comprehend, interpret and discuss the concept of 重男轻女 from the video clip and the article.
2. Students can share their reflections and perspective about 重男轻女.
3. Students can complete an online survey, discuss the results, and present to the whole class.
4. Students can interpret the comic about gender inequality.
5. Student can identify actions that are considered to be gender inequality in different countries from the video clips.
6. Students can propose resolutions to problems of gender inequality.
7. Students can present their findings about gender inequality to their peers in written and oral formats.

Task 1   Son Preference in China   重男轻女

Communicative Mode: Interpretive and Interpersonal

Step 1: Please watch the video until 1:22. 请你看下面的视频，看到 1 分 22 秒。
https://www.youtube.com/watch?v=WlstyQ1pPMk

Step 2: Disuses the meaning of the video with your partner. 跟你的同学讨论这个小视频的意义。

Step 3: Watch the video again, then complete the table below according to the content of the video. 再看一次视频，并根据视频内容完成下面的表格。

哪些是男孩子在家里的待遇？哪些是女孩子在家里的待遇？

待遇	男孩子	女孩子
出国留学		
卖房子		
砸锅卖铁		
倾家荡产		
上大学，家里不肯出钱		
早上吃早餐吃泡饭		
早上吃早餐吃火腿加鸡蛋		
早上吃早餐喝白开水		
早上吃早餐喝果汁牛奶		
洗碗擦地扫地		
舍不得买复习资料给孩子		

Step 4: In a group of 3 or 4, discuss the following question, then each group take turns to report to the class. 三到四个同学一组，讨论下面的问题。然后每组轮流报告。

1. 视频里，妈妈对女儿说："我们只负责养你到18岁，你以后还要嫁人，到老了，我们也不需要你养。"你同意这样的想法吗？为什么？这跟一般美国家庭父母的观念一样吗？
2. 视频里，女儿两次对妈妈说："你嫌弃我是个女孩，为什么要生我？"；"你生我又不想养我，你生我干什么？难道就给你当出气筒吗？"你们认为为什么妈妈还要生下她？你同情这个女孩吗？她说的这些话有道理吗？

Task 2　Why Do the Chinese Prefer Sons?　中国人为什么重男轻女？

Communicative Mode: Interpretive, Interpersonal and Presentational

Step 1: Please share your ideas with your partner. 请跟你的同学分享你的想法。
你认为重男轻女的原因是什么？

Step 2: Please read the following article and find out the reasons why Chinese prefer sons. 请阅读下面的文章，找出中国人重男轻女的原因。
http://kuaibao.qq.com/s/20180303A0JZI200?refer=spider

中国人为什么重男轻女？
1.
2.
3.
4.
5.
6.

Step 3: Discuss the following questions with your classmates. 跟你的同学讨论下面的问题。

1. 这六个原因当中，你认为哪些是合理的？哪些是不合理的？请说明理由。
2. 这些原因跟美国的价值观有冲突吗？美国重男轻女或重女轻男的原因是什么？请举例说明。

Task 3　Online Survey　在线调查

Communicative Mode: Interpretive, Interpersonal, and Presentational

Step1: Please complete the survey before the class. 请在上课前完成下面的问卷调查。

Instructional Strategies:
The instructor creates an online survey through Survey Monkey or Google Forms.

1. 在美国，男女平等吗？
   ○ 十分平等
   ○ 重男轻女
   ○ 重女轻男
2. 在美国，你认为在哪个方面男女还不太平等？（可多选）
   ○ 家庭地位　　　○ 社会地位
   ○ 教育机会　　　○ 工作机会
   ○ 工资收入

3. 在美国，父母对待儿子和女儿在哪些方面不一样？（可多选）
   ○ 培养兴趣　　　　　○ 物质享受
   ○ 教育升学　　　　　○ 未来期待
   ○ 情绪管理　　　　　○ 礼貌态度
   ○ 服装打扮

4. 在美国，抚养男孩跟女孩的费用一样吗？
   ○ 抚养男孩女孩的费用一样
   ○ 抚养男孩的费用高于女孩
   ○ 抚养女孩的费用高于男孩

5. 请对上一道题你的选择举例说明（简答题）

6. 在你的家里，你的父母对儿子跟女儿的要求一样吗？
   ○ 对儿子女儿的要求一样
   ○ 对儿子的要求比较高
   ○ 对女儿的要求比较高

7. 请对上一道题举例说明，你的父母对儿子跟女儿的要求有哪些一样或者不一样的地方？（简答题）

8. 在你看来，男孩跟女孩一样让父母担心吗？
   ○ 男孩跟女孩一样让父母担心
   ○ 男孩比女孩更容易让父母担心
   ○ 女孩比男孩更容易让父母担心

9. 如果以后你有孩子，你更希望你的第一个孩子是男孩子还是女孩子？
   ○ 男孩子　　　　　○ 女孩子　　　　　○ 都可以

10. 请对上一道题具体说明，为什么你更希望你的第一个孩子是男孩或者女孩，或者都可以？（简答题）

Step 2: Work in pairs to share your answers and present your answers to the whole class.
跟你的同学一起讨论你们填写的调查问卷，然后向全班报告。

Instructional Strategies:
The instructor shows the results of the class by providing charts in percentage form and ask the students to present results compared to their own answers. (Pick 2-3 out of 10 results to present depending on the numbers of students).

Suggested Words and Structures:

An organization/place ＋ 对 ＋ topic of a survey ＋ 进行了调查	(An organization/place) ...... conducted a survey on a topic
The number of respondents ＋ 参与调查	(The number of respondents) ...... participated in the survey
百分之 X	X Percent
人 ＋ 表示 ＋ opinions or stance	Someone expressed that ...... (opinion or stance)
调查数据 ＋ 显示 ＋ the result of a survey	Data of the survey shows that ...... (result of the survey)
其中	among
……占很大的比例	...... has high percentage on
将近 / 大约	almost/around
绝大多数	overwhelming majority

Task 4 Boy or Girl: What Do People Prefer in Different Countries?
不同国家的人重男轻女还是重女轻男？

Communicative Mode: Interpretive, Interpersonal, and Presentational

Step 1: Choose your answers. 选一选，说一说。
你认为下面这6个国家，哪几个国家重男轻女/重女轻男？
A. 瑞典　　　B. 加拿大　　　C. 西班牙
D. 乌克兰　　E. 日本　　　　F. 韩国

Step 2: Please watch the video clip that is assigned to your group. Each group represents one country and completes the following table based on the assigned video clip. 请看老师布置给你的视频片段。每一组代表一个国家，然后根据你观看的视频片段完成下面的表格。

https://www.youtube.com/watch?v=cv2zrNV4psg

瑞典（2:50-4:38）　　加拿大（4:38-6:05）　　乌克兰（11:04-12:40）
日本（12:40-14:15）　韩国（14:17-16:16）　　美国（16:17-17:37）
西班牙（17:37-19:00）

国家	重男轻女还是重女轻男	有哪些体现，请具体说明

Step 3: Share your answers with the class. While one group is presenting, other students should take notes and complete the following table. 跟你的同学分享你的答案。当一组同学报告时，其他同学记笔记完成下面的表格。

国家	重男轻女还是重女轻男	具体说明

Step 4: Please complete the following table and then elaborate your perspectives. 请完成下面的表格，然后详细说明你的看法。

你认为下面的几个叙述合理不合理？

	合理	不合理
对男孩女孩应该培养不同的兴趣		
对男孩女孩的未来应该有不同的期待		
女孩应该比男孩有更好的物质享受		
应该教育男孩有责任心、更独立、更坚强		
应该教育女孩温柔、体贴、善解人意		
女孩嫁人嫁得好比工作做得好更重要		

Task 5 Who Does the Housework? 谁做家务？

Communicative Mode: Interpersonal and Presentational

Step1: Please complete the following table. 请你完成下面的表格。

在你的家庭中，下面的这些家事主要由谁负担？

	爸爸 > 妈妈	妈妈 > 爸爸
买菜		
做饭		
洗碗		
洗衣服		
洗车		
收拾房间		
付水电费		
给孩子买衣服		
接送孩子参加课外活动		
去学校参加家长会		
……		
……		

Step 2: Add more items to the list and discuss with your classmates. 在表格上加一些新的内容，然后和你的同学讨论。

Step 3: Please answer the following questions. Share your answers and discuss in your group. 请回答下面的问题，跟你的同学分享、讨论你们的答案。

1. 在你的家庭里，谁做的家务最多？
2. 你认为这样的家庭分工公平不公平？
3. 你常常帮你的父母做家务吗？你做什么家务？
4. 如果以后你有家庭，你会如何分配家务？

Step 4: Watch the video clip until 0:28 and answer the following questions. 看下面的视频到 28 秒。

https://www.youtube.com/watch?v=hdVxUV7HQEg

1. 这个视频中，采访的问题是什么？
2. 这个人同意不同意当家庭主夫？他的看法是什么？你同意不同意他的看法？
3. 你认为在中国，有多少男性接受家庭主夫的观念？有多少女性接受家庭主夫的观念？

Step 5: Watch the video from 2:26-2:32 and answer the following questions. 看视频的 2 分 26 秒到 2 分 32 秒，并回答下面的问题。

1. 在视频的最后，有多少男性受访者接受家庭主夫的观念？多少女性不接受家庭主夫的观念？
2. 这个采访结果跟你想象中的一样吗？
3. 你想不想做家庭主夫/家庭主妇？你支持不支持你的丈夫/妻子当家庭主夫/家庭主妇？为什么？
4. 在你的中文班上，有多少男孩子想做家庭主夫？有多少女孩子想做家庭主妇？多少人支持自己的丈夫/妻子当家庭主夫/家庭主妇？

Task 6   Gender Equality at Workplace   职场男女平等

Communicative Mode: Interpretive, Interpersonal, and Presentational

Step 1: Please interpret the comic below. Then discuss the meaning of this comic with your partner. 请你看下面的漫画，跟你的同学讨论这张漫画的意义。

Step 2: Please post a picture or comic related to gender inequality on Padlet. Then describe and interpret the picture/comic to the whole class. 请你找一张有关男女不平等的图片或漫画，放在 Padlet 上。然后跟全班同学描述这张图片或漫画的意义。

Step 3: Please complete the following checklist before class. 请在课前完成下面的表格。

在美国，下面的这些职业中男性多还是女性多？

职业	男性多于女性	女性多于男性
医生		
护士		
幼儿园老师		
美容师		
电脑工程师		
飞行员		
快递员		
前台服务员		
建筑工人		
汽车修理工		
*Note: Add more occupations if necessary		
1		
2		
3		

Step 4: Exchange and compare the results of your self-checklist with your peers. 跟你的同学交换、比较你们的答案。

Step 5: Discuss the following questions based on the results. And then share your opinions with the whole class. 根据你们的答案讨论下面的问题，然后跟全班同学分享你们的看法。

1. 你跟你朋友的看法一样吗？有哪个/哪些看法不一样？为什么？
2. 你们认为在美国哪些职业男性要多于女性，哪些职业女性要多于男性？
3. 你们认为这些男性多于女性的职业，有哪些共同点？
4. 你们认为这些女性多于男性的职业，有哪些共同点？
5. 你赞成不赞成"不同性别有不同社会分工"的说法？为什么？

Task 7 Gender Inequality in the World 世界上的男女不平等情况

Communicative Mode: Interpersonal and Presentational

Step 1: There are many examples of gender inequality existing in the world today. The teacher divides the whole class into groups. Each group determines the selected country. 大家分成几个组，每组确定一个国家。

Step 2: Analyze the current status of gender inequality in the country. Identify 2-3 problems or challenges. 分析这个国家男女不平等的情况。指出2-3个问题或是挑战。

Step 3: In response to the issues, the committee members discuss the solutions and an action plan. 针对这些问题，小组成员讨论解决措施和改进方案。

Step 4: Give an oral presentation. 向全班报告你们的方案。

Suggested Words and Structures:

针对……问题	in response to the issue ……
一方面……另一方面	on the one hand , …….. on the other hand ……
在……方面	in the aspect of ……
首先…其次……再次……最后	firstly…secondly …… thirdly …… finally
提出	to raise; to propse
建议	to suggest
为了……	in order to ……
解决问题	solve the problem
采取……措施	take measures; take step
与此同时	in the meantime
毫无疑问	undoubtedly
换句话说	in other words
总而言之	in conclusion

Rubric for Oral Presentation

Visual Evidence (10 pts)	
9-10	Demonstrating efforts in compiling and organizing visual aids
7-8	Recognizable efforts in compiling and organizing visual aids
4-6	Some efforts in compiling and organizing visual aids
0-3	Minimal efforts in compiling and organizing visual aids
Organization and Content (20 pts)	
16-20	Fully describing the present, identifying current problems and challenges; proposing feasible and justifiable resolutions to challenges
11-15	Describing the present, identifying current problems and challenges; proposing acceptable resolutions to challenges
6-10	Partially describing the present, identifying current problems and challenges; proposing the solutions that are not sound or justifiable to challenges
0-5	Lacking a lot of information about the present, as well as current problems and challenges; no justifiable or feasible resolutions
Accuracy of Language: Sentence Patterns, Word Choices and Pronunciation (50 pts)	
45-50	No or few errors in sentence patterns and word choices; achieving goals of detailed descriptions, persuasion, and problem-solving
35-44	Several errors in sentence patterns and word choices; mostly achieving goals of detailed descriptions, persuasion, and problem-solving
20-34	Some errors in sentence patterns and word choices; partially achieving goals of detailed descriptions, persuasion, and problem-solving
0-19	Errors prevalent in sentence patterns and word choices; not achieving goals of detailed descriptions, persuasion, and problem-solving
Preparation and Efforts: Pre-class and In-class Preparation and Efforts (10 pts)	
9-10	Strong indication of solid preparation and rehearsals; demonstrating great efforts; having great fluency and frequent eye contact
6-8	Some indication of rehearsals; recognizable efforts; generally smooth pacing with some eye contact during a presentation
4-6	Insufficient rehearsals with limited efforts; halting speech and eye contact during a presentation
0-3	No or little indication of rehearsals; few efforts; disconnected speech; no eye contact and reading from a script

*Note: The task can turn into a presentational writing task with slight adjustment.

Chapter 3

Personal and Public Identities　个人与社群认同

Unit 3: Dating for You and Me　约会你和我

Contributor: Miao-fen Tseng
Proficiency Level: Intermediate-Low to Intermediate-Mid
Instructional Time: 8-10 hours
Can-Do Statements:
1. Students can create and describe their online profile with personal background information and characteristics.
2. Students can ask questions and engage in conversations to gather information about personal background information and traits.
3. Students can express and explain one's preferences of choosing an ideal "partner" after a face-to-face date.

Task 1　Speed Dating　闪电约会

Communicative Mode: Interpretive, Interpersonal, and Presentational

Step 1: Use the following table to complete your own personal information before class.
上课前，用下面的表格填写你的个人信息。

性别		身高	
体重		星座	
血型		属相	
专业/学历		爱好	
体型		外貌	
性格		收入	
工作		宗教信仰	
有没有车		有没有住房	

Step 2: Bring the completed table to class for the speed dating activity. In class, exchange your information with three other "dates". Fill in the following table of your three "dates". 把你填好的表格带到课上，和三位同学口头交换信息（男同学和女同学练习，女同学和男同学练习）。然后把他们的信息填入下面的表格。

怎么问问题？
1. 你是男的还是女的？
2. 你多高？多重？
3. 你是什么血型？你是什么属相（你是属什么的）？
4. 你的专业是什么？你的最高学历是什么？你有什么爱好？
5. 你的体型怎么样？你的外貌怎么样？你的性格怎么样？
6. 你一年/一个月的收入是多少？收入高不高？
7. 你做什么工作？
8. 你有没有宗教信仰？你信（仰）什么宗教？

性别	身高
体重	星座
血型	属相
专业/学历	爱好
体型	外貌
性格	收入
工作	宗教信仰
有没有车	有没有住房

Step 3: Briefly introduce your "dates" and tell the classes if they meet your criteria. 向全班同学介绍你的"约会对象"，并告诉大家他们是否符合你的标准。

Checklist for Interpersonal Communication

Completion of the table of personal information
1   2   3   4   5   6   7   8   9   10

Rich vocabulary and expressions in questions and responses
1   2   3   4   5   6   7   8   9   10

A variety of structures in questions and responses
1   2   3   4   5   6   7   8   9   10

Frequent turn-taking, fluency, and comprehensible pronunciation
1   2   3   4   5   6   7   8   9   10

Instructional Strategies:

Instructors may organize three rounds of speed dating in class and ask students to report about their partner after the end of each round.

Suggested Key Words and Expressions:

学历	xuélì	highest degree
大学硕士	dàxué shuòshì	master's degree
博士	bóshì	Ph.D.
外貌	wàimào	appearance
年轻貌美，长得很像电影明星	niánqīng màoměi, zhǎngde hěnxiàng diàn yǐng míngxīng	长得很 + adjective
性格	xìnggé	personality
内向	nèixiàng	introvert
外向	wàixiàng	extrovert
害羞	hàixiū	shy
活泼	huópō	lively, viracious
大方	dàfang	generous/natural
文静	wénjìng	quiet
温柔	wēnróu	tender
开朗	kāilǎng	outgoing with optimism
热情	rèqíng	warm-hearted with enthusiasm about helping friends

爱交朋友	ài jiāo péngyǒu	love making new friends
完美主义者	wánměizhǔyìzhě	perfectionist
乐观	lèguān	optimistic
幽默（爱说笑话）	yōumò（ài shuō xiàohua）	humorous
独立	dúlì	independent
体贴	tǐtiē	considerate
体型	tǐxíng	body type, figure
高大	gāodà	tall and strong
胖	pàng	large
瘦	shòu	skinny
瘦小	shòuxiǎo	short and skinny
不胖不瘦	búpàngbúshòu	neither too big nor too skinny
苗条	miáotiáo	slim, in a great shape
高矮	gāo'ǎi	height
不高不矮	bùgāobù'ǎi	average height
收入	shōurù	income
每个月……美元，年薪……美元	měigèyuè …… měiyuán, niánxīn …… měiyuán	monthly/yearly salary
住房	zhùfáng	housing
没有房子（＝无房）	méiyǒufángzi (=wúfáng)	not owning a house
租房子	zūfángzǐ	rent a house
有房	yǒufáng	have own house
宗教信仰	zōngjiào xìnyǎng	religious belief
基督教	jīdūjiào	Christianity
天主教	tiānzhǔjiào	Catholicism
伊斯兰教教	huíjiào	Islamism
佛教	fójiào	Buddhism
没有＝无	méiyǒu=wú	Not ……

Add "徒" right after each religion, then it becomes "a person who believes in a certain type of religion."
我 信 / 信仰 (I believe in) + one of the above religious names

Task 2 Online Dating 线上约会

Communicative Mode: Interpretive and Interpersonal

Step 1: Before class, view the website "中国同城约会网" (http://yuehui.163.com/) to get a sense of what a personal profile may look like and what kind of information is needed. 上课前，请看中国同城约会网，了解"爱的档案"一般包含什么信息。

Step 2: Imagine who you will be and what you will do 5-10 years from now. Create your personal profile, including 1) a title, and 2) a table with more detailed personal information below. 想想你自己5到10年以后的样子，建立爱的档案，包括1）标题；2）一个有下面内容的表格：

性别	身高
体重	星座
血型	专业
爱好	外貌
性格	体型
属相	学历
收入	工作
宗教信仰	有没有车
有没有住房	

Instructional Strategies:
Remind the students that this is an imaginary task, and their information cannot be identical to that of speed dating in Task 1.

Step 3: Compose your date selection criteria (include it in your profile) with a minimum of 150-200 characters. The statement should include but is not limited to the following information. 写一个150到200字的择偶声明（也放在爱的档案里），要至少包含下面的信息。

爱的表白／自我介绍／我的特征（love statements/self-intro/personal characteristics）
我理想的对象／梦中情人／白马王子／另一半／人生伴侣（descriptions and standards of your dream spouse/partner）

Instructional Strategies:
If circumstances arise, such as transgender or students showing homosexual preference, teachers shall respect their identities and preferences.

Step 4: Upload your personal profile and statement to the designated site online. 把你的个人信息上传到指定的网站。

Instructional Strategies:
1. It is highly recommended that instructor remind the students do not upload their profile on the real dating website in order to protect their privacy.
2. Remind the students that they can only include a nickname in their profiles. The instructor will only reveal their names after the students have made their dating choices.

Step 5: Read through personal profiles and statements created by all the friends of the opposite gender and choose your ideal match to prepare for the face-to-face dating activity in class. 读一读所有异性朋友的爱的档案和择偶声明，选一个理想的，为面对面约会做准备。

Rubric for the Online Personal Profile (Writing Presentation)

Categories	Excellent	Very good	Good	Fair	Needs great improvement
Information (10 pts.)	Includes a wealth of info. about dating process: speed dating, blind online dating, and face-to-face dating. (8-10pts.)	Includes most info. about dating process: speed dating, blind online dating, and face-to-face dating. (6-8pts.)	Includes some info. about dating process: speed dating, blind online dating, and face-to-face dating. (4-6pts.)	Includes limited info. about dating process: speed dating, blind online dating, and face-to-face dating (2-4pts.)	Lacks needed info. (0-2pts.)
Language Use (20 pts.)	Mastery of target structures and key voc. (16-20pts.)	Most appropriate use of target structures and key voc. (12-16pts.)	Some appropriate use of target structures and key voc. (8-12pts.)	Limited use of appropriate target structures and key voc. (4-8pts.)	Pervasive inappropriate use of target structures and key voc. (0-4pts.)
Organization and Thoughts (10 pts.)	Well-organized and well-delivered thoughts (8-10pts.)	Appropriately organized and clear thoughts (6-8pts.)	Acceptable organization and generally understandable thoughts (4-6pts.)	Mostly inappropriate organization and unclear thoughts (2-4pts.)	Disorganized and unclear thoughts (0-2pts.)
Writing Conventions (10 pts.)	Meets all requirements (8-10pts.)	Meets most requirements (6-8pts.)	Meets some requirements (4-6pts.)	Meets limited requirements (2-4pts.)	Meets none or 1-2 requirements (0-2pts.)

Task 3   Face-to-Face Dating   见面约会（女孩选男孩）

Communicative Mode: Interpretive, Interpersonal, and Presentational

Step 1: Before the face-to-face dating activity, please complete the checklist and bring the hardcopy to class. 面对面约会以前，请把下面的备忘填好，把需要带的资料打印好带到课上。

Girls' Checklist Before Class
(   ) I have viewed all boys' profiles and statements.
(   ) I have chosen one dream boyfriend.
(   ) I have read through his description and learn all about him.
(   ) I have printed out his profile and statement and will bring it to class.
(   ) I have prepared my 1-minute oral presentation to explain how and why I choose certain person.

Boys' Checklist Before Class
(   ) I have printed out my profile and statement and will bring it to class.
(   ) I have practiced out loud and best prepared for the information that I included in my profile and statement.

Step 2: Each girl has one minute to present their choices. 每位女孩子用一分钟时间介绍她的选择。

Step 3: The instructor will reveal the real names of the boys from their profiles. The girls can now make changes and tell the class why she made such change. 老师会把爱的档案给大家看，让女孩子这时候知道每个档案是班上哪个男孩子的。女孩子这时候可以换人，并告诉大家为什么换人，为什么不换。

Step 4: "Date" with the person you chose. Referring to his profile, ask him questions to verify whether he is the right person for you. The ones who are not chosen will practice in a group for a final personal statement in the next stage. 跟你选的男孩子面对面约会：看他的爱的档案，问他很多问题，看看你是不是真的喜欢他。没选上的男孩子互相自我介绍，准备再次展示自己。

Step 5: The girls present their answers to the following questions: whether he is the right person? If so, why? After "dating" him in class, will you "date" him in the future? Do you really like him? If so, why? 请女孩子报告：他是你真的想约会

的人吗？为什么？跟他面对面约会以后，你还想再跟他约会吗？他真的是你喜欢的男孩子吗？为什么？

Step 6: Each boy, who was not selected can introduce himself (love profile) for the last time. 没被选上的男孩子用一分钟的时间介绍自己的爱的档案。最后的机会！！！

Step 7: After hearing the boys' final statements, the girls can reconsider their choices and present in class about their decisions and rationale. 女孩子听了介绍以后，现在再考虑考虑，告诉大家你喜欢谁，要不要改变决定，想跟谁约会。

Rubric for Speaking

1. Rich Information
   1 2 3 4 5 6 7 8 9 10

2. Appropriate Use of Structures and Vocabulary
   1 2 3 4 5 6 7 8 9 10

3. Inclusion of Additional Expressions
   1 2 3 4 5 6 7 8 9 10

4. Pronunciation & Fluency
   1 2 3 4 5 6 7 8 9 10

Task 4   Face-to-Face Dating   见面约会（男孩选女孩）

Communicative Mode: Interpretive, Interpersonal, and Presentational

Instructional Strategies:

Please be noted that Task 3 and Task 4 follow exactly the same procedure. The only difference is that in Task 3 girls choose boys, but in Task 4 boys choose girls.

Step 1: Before the face-to-face dating activity, please complete the following appropriate checklist and bring the hard copy to class. 面对面约会以前，请把下面的备忘填好，把需要带的资料打印好带到课上。

Boys' Checklist Before Class
(   ) I have viewed all girls' profiles and statements.
(   ) I have chosen one dream girlfriend.
(   ) I have read through her description and learn all about her.
(   ) I have printed out her profile and statement and will bring it to class.
(   ) I have prepared my 1-minute oral presentation to explain how and why I choose certain person.

Girls' Checklist Before Class
(   ) I have printed out my profile and statement and will bring it to class.
(   ) I have practiced out loud and best prepared for the information that I included in my profile and statement.

Step 2: Each boy has one minute to present their choices. 每位男孩子用一分钟时间介绍他的选择。

Step 3: The instructor will reveal the real names of the girls from their profiles. The boys can now make changes and tell the class why he made such change. 老师会把爱的档案给大家看，让男孩子知道每个档案是班上哪个女孩子的。这时候男孩子可以换人，并告诉大家为什么换人，为什么不换。

Step 4: "Date" with the person you chose before. Referring to her profile, ask her questions to verify whether she is the right person for you. The ones who are not chosen will practice in a group for a final personal statement in the next stage. 跟你选的女孩子面对面约会：看她的爱的档案，问她很多问题，看看你是不是真的喜欢她。没选上的女孩子互相自我介绍，准备再次展示自己。

Step 5: The boys present their answers to the following questions in class: whether she is the right person? If so, why? After "dating" her in class, will you "date" her in the future? Do you really like her? If so, why? 请男孩子报告：她是你真的想约会的人吗？为什么？跟她面对面约会以后，你还想再跟她约会吗？她真的是你喜欢的女孩子吗？为什么？

Step 6: Each girl who was not picked can introduce herself (love profile) for the last time. 每位女孩子用一分钟的时间介绍自己的爱的档案。最后的机会！！！

Step 7: After hearing the girls' final statements, boys reconsider their choices and present in class about their decisions and rationale. 男孩子听了介绍以后，现在再考虑考虑，告诉大家你喜欢谁，要不要改变决定，想跟谁约会。

Rubric for Speaking

1. Rich Information
   1 2 3 4 5 6 7 8 9 10

2. Appropriate Use of Structures and Vocabulary
   1 2 3 4 5 6 7 8 9 10

3. Inclusion of Additional Expressions
   1 2 3 4 5 6 7 8 9 10

4. Pronunciation & Fluency
   1 2 3 4 5 6 7 8 9 10

Task 5   My Dating Experiences   我的约会经历

Communicative Mode: Interpretive and Presentational

Step 1: Refer to the information that you have included in your statement and your preferred partner's profile, summarize key information in an essay on your dating experience. 根据你的约会经历和你的档案、择偶标准，写一篇总结的文章。

Required information in THREE paragraphs:

Paragraph ONE: Self-introduction
In other words, describe your background information — yourself now, and yourself in 5 or 10 years from now.

Paragraph TWO: 1) Criteria of your preferred partner, 2) experiences of your face-to-face dating or your online dating, 3) explain the reasons for your choices.

Guided questions:
1. 你上课的时候跟谁约会？是面对面的约会还是在网上约会？
2. 在网上约会的时候，你一共看了几个人的档案？是男孩子的档案还是女孩子的档案？你觉得这些档案怎么样？
3. 你先在网上约会，然后才见面约会。你最后选谁见面约会？为什么？

Paragraph THREE: Your wish and future plan
Guided questions:
你想 / 希望 / 要什么时候结婚？你觉得什么时候结婚最好？想 / 会 / 希望在哪儿结婚？去哪儿蜜月旅行？为什么？怎么去？……

Rubric for Presentational Writing

1. **Information:** Follow instructions and include all required information about the guided questions (15 pts.)

   Competent   Near competent   Partially competent   Incompetent
   (14-15 pts.)   (11-13 pts.)   (6-10 pts.)   (0-5 pts.)

2. **Organization & Thoughts:** Includes three paragraphs to express ideas and thoughts coherently (15 pts.)

   Competent   Near competent   Partially competent   Incompetent
   (14-15 pts.)   (11-13 pts.)   (6-10 pts.)   (0-5 pts.)

3. **Structures:** Incorporate a variety of well-formed structures (40 pts.)

   Competent   Near competent   Partially competent   Incompetent
   (36-40 pts.)   (30-35 pts.)   (20-29 pts.)   (0-19 pts.)

4. **Expansion of key words and expressions:** Incorporate additional key words and expressions that you learned from the pink love table and the love profile created by your peers (30 pts.)

   Competent   Near competent   Partially competent   Incompetent
   (26-30 pts.)   (21-25 pts.)   (15-20 pts.)   (0-15 pts.)

Step 2: Peer learning: read your peer's essay and answer the related questions based on his/her essay. 读一读你同学的文章，回答相关问题。

Instructional Strategy 1:
At the end of the semester, the teacher will select several well-written essays for students to do peer learning as part of the final exam. The following is a sample essay that was identical to the content of the handwritten essay except for the added glossary that was created and highlighted for the purpose of peer learning.

Instructional Strategy 2:
Task-supported or task-based learning is intrinsically motivating, but since authentic materials are selected and organized by teachers themselves, the sequence of word

expressions and grammatical structures sometimes could be challenging and need to be carefully spiraled and recycled to consolidate learning. The essay writing of the mid-term that is spiraled up and re-used for the end-of-semester final exam is a good example of student-centered peer learning and recycled learning materials created by learners themselves.

Sample essay for peer learning:

您好，我叫昊天。我二十六岁，属猴。我的星座是射手座（1）。我是O型血型。我的专业是电气工程（2），最高学历是硕士（3）。我的身高是一百七十三厘米，体重七十五公斤。我没有宗教信仰（4）。我不但很灵敏（5），而且很幽默（6），很周到（7）。虽然我没有电影明星那么帅，可是我的外貌不错，体型也不太胖，不太瘦。我的收入是一年十万美元，是一个电气工程师。我有很多爱好：除了打羽毛球以外，我还很喜欢听音乐，在咖啡馆放松（8），还有做菜。我有车，还有一个公寓。

因为我觉得外貌不太重要，所以我不要一位很漂亮的女孩子。可是，我最喜欢很酷，很冷静（9），很大方（10），很聪明的女孩子，因为我想跟我的女朋友一起工作。因为我不太外向（11），所以我希望找到一个不太外向的女朋友。最重要的是，她得喜欢吃很好吃的菜。如果她很会做菜，应该很好（12），不过如果她不会做，我可以教她。我星期三上课以前先在网上约会。在网上约会的时候，我一共看了八个爱的档案（13）。我觉得这些爱的档案很好看。然后，我星期三上课的时候跟溥莉面对面约会。我对她的印象很好，因为她是厨师（14），很会做菜。再说，她也又活泼（15），又乐观（16）。可是，她说她喜欢在饭馆约会，不喜欢在咖啡馆约会。我喜欢在咖啡放松，所以我觉得我得选别人约会。我最后选Yuling。因为她也喜欢在咖啡馆放松，所以我觉得她比溥莉合适。

我要找到工作以后才结婚，因为我会有一笔钱。我觉得认识一年以后结婚最好。我希望在曼谷（17）结婚，因为在曼谷菜很好吃，也很便宜。我想坐飞机去夏威夷（18）蜜月旅行（19），因为我觉得在海滩（20）最浪漫（21）。我希望有两个孩子，一个儿子和一个女儿。我希望有很幸福（22）的家，我要帮太太做菜，不要让她太辛苦（23）。

Sample questions:
1. 他长得不错，可是没有电影明星那么好看。(对/错)
2. 他觉得女孩子是不是漂亮不重要。(对/错)
3. 他喜欢比较外向的女孩子。(对/错)
4. 他的女朋友一定得喜欢做菜才行。(对/错)
5. 你觉得几岁结婚最合适？希望在哪儿结婚，蜜月旅行？

Sample vocabulary list:

1. 射手座 — Shèshǒu zuò — Sagittarius
2. 电气工程 — diànqì gōngchéng — electrical engineering
3. 灵敏 — língmǐn — sensitive/keen/understanding
4. 幽默 — yōumò — humorous
5. 周到 — zhōudào — thoughtful
6. 放松 — fàngsōng — chill/relax
7. 冷静 — lěngjìng — cool, level-headed
8. 大方 — dàfāng — natural/genuine
9. 外向 — wàixiàng — extroverted
10. X 为 Y 会做任何事情 — X wèi Y huì zuò rènhé shìqing — X will do anything for Y
11. 爱的档案 — ài de dǎng'àn — love profiles
12. 厨师 — chúshī — chef
13. 活泼 — huópō — lively
14. 乐观 — lèguān — optimistic
15. 曼谷 — Màngǔ — Bangkok
16. 夏威夷 — Xiàwēiyí — Hawaii
17. 蜜月旅行 — mìyuè lǚxíng — Honeymoon
18. 海滩 — hǎitān — beach
19. 浪漫 — làngmàn — romantic
20. 幸福 — xìngfú — happy
21. 辛苦 — xīnkǔ — work hard

Suggested Structures:

我希望我未来（wèi lái, future）的男/女朋友……
有没有 + something 没关系/不重要（not that important），我觉得最重要的是 something OR 我觉得 something 最重要
如果……，就会…….（就 is required in the 2nd clause）
越来越 + adjective /（不）喜欢
A 比 B + adjective（or various structures to make comparisons）
A 跟 B（不）一样
我跟 somebody 约会
我跟 somebody 见面
我对 somebody 的印象最好
约会完了以后，我选（xuǎn, choose）somebody

Chapter 4

Beauty and Esthetics   美学艺术

Unit 1: Tell the Story of an Advertisement   看广告说故事

Contributor: Miao-fen Tseng
Proficiency Level: Intermediate-Mid to Intermediate-High
Instructional Time: 4-5 hours
Can-Do Statements:

1. Students can identify a sequence of actions in accordance with the development of the story line in the video.
2. Students can communicate with peers to generate needed information in alignment with the content of the video.
3. Students can present a dialogue or a story in alignment with the development of the story line in the video.

Task 1   A McDonald's Advertisement   麦当劳广告

Communicative Mode: Interpretive and Interpersonal

Step 1: In class, watch the following video until 0:35. 在课上看下面的视频，看到 35 秒。
https://www.youtube.com/watch?v=UBAF65omIs4&feature=player_embedded

Instructional Strategies:
The instructor pauses the video at the 35 second mark and asks the entire class to predict what the boy would say and why he runs back.

Step 2: Discuss your predictions and guesses with the whole class. After the discussion, continue to watch the video until the end to see what happens next. 讨论并猜一猜后面会发生什么。讨论之后，把视频看完。

Step 3: Watch the video again. Then complete the following task to describe what you see. Discuss your answers with your partner and tell the entire story based on the correct sequences. 从头再看一遍视频，并完成下面的练习。和你的同学讨论，并试着按顺序把故事讲出来。

91

Use 1, 2, 3, 4, 5, 6, 7, 8, 9 to identify a sequence of 9 actions that you see from the video.

(　　) 小丽和小华在火车站依依不舍,紧紧地抱在一起,不想说再见。
(　　) 有一天,雪下得很大,天气冷得不得了,火车站到处都是雪。
(　　) 火车慢慢地开走了。
(　　) 小华送小丽上火车。
(　　) 小华急急忙忙地跑回去找小丽。
(　　) 小丽坐在火车里,小华在火车外面,隔着窗户依依不舍地看着小丽。
(　　) 小华摸摸口袋,突然想起来有一样东西在小丽那儿。
(　　) 小华给女孩一件厚厚的外套。
(　　) 看到小丽的时候,小华隔着窗户比手画脚,告诉小丽有一样东西在她那儿。
(10) 小丽……

Answer keys:
1. 有一天,雪下得很大,天气冷得不得了,火车站到处都是雪。
2. 小丽和小华在火车站依依不舍,紧紧地抱在一起,不想说再见。
3. 小华送小丽上火车。
4. 小丽坐在火车里,小华在火车外面,隔着窗户依依不舍地看着小丽。
5. 小华给女孩一件厚厚的外套。
6. 火车慢慢地开走了。
7. 小华摸摸口袋,突然想起来有一样东西在小丽那儿。
8. 小华急急忙忙地跑回去找小丽。
9. 看到小丽的时候,隔着窗户比手划脚,告诉小丽有一样东西在她那儿。
10. 小丽……

Task 2　Plot Discussion　故事情节讨论

Communicative Mode: Interpersonal and Presentational

Step 1: Based on the video in the previous task, discuss the following questions in a group of 2-3. Take notes of your answers. 根据任务1的视频,两到三位同学一组讨论下面的问题,讨论的时候记笔记。

WHEN: 这个故事发生在什么时候?什么季节?天气怎么样?
WHO: 故事里有谁?几个人?他们几岁?长得怎么样?性格怎么样?
WHERE: 在哪儿?是什么样的地方?吵不吵?安静吗?是不是有很多人?
WHAT: 他们在一起做什么?说什么话?
WHY: 他们为什么在一起?他们的关系怎么样?男孩子在电影最后为什么跑回去找那个女孩子?这个结果让人很意外(unexpected; beyond expectation)吗?
WHAT: 这个广告主要的目的(mùdì, purpose)是什么?想告诉观众(看广告的人)

什么？如果你是导演（拍这个广告的人），想给这个广告取一个不一样的名字，你会取什么名字？为什么取这个名字？如果你想改变这个电影最后的故事，你想怎么改变？

Step 2: Share your discussion to the whole class. 跟全班报告你们的讨论结果。

Task 3　Narrate and Act the Story　故事旁白和表演

Communicative Mode: Interpersonal and Presentational

Option 1: Narration 旁白
Connect and organize all responses to the above questions to create a story narration of "麦当劳广告" comprised of a string of sentences. Use the following connective structures and the detailing devices (appropriate adjectives, detailed information, and your own comments) to enrich the story by taking account of what you have discussed in Task 2. 根据之前的讨论，请你设计一个旁白，用能承前启后的句子描述"麦当劳广告"的故事情节。请使用下面的句型和连词进行表达，并且加入描述细节的词（恰当的形容词，细节信息和你的评论）使你的旁白更丰富。

Sentence 1……然后, sentence 2 (2 consecutive actions)
Verbal phrase 1 以后，verbal phrase 2 (two consecutive actions)
Sentence 1……于是 (therefore), sentence 2 (cause and effect relationship)
最后，complete sentence.

Instructional Strategies:
Each student presents the story narration either in spoken or written form. Another highly recommended option is to invite students to narrate the story line while the instructor plays the video. Remember to minimize the background music, so the students' voice will be heard clearly.

Option 2: Acting 表演

Step 1: The commercial ad has three segments that may involve the dialogue between the boy and girl. In pairs/groups, please create three short dialogues in correspondence with the three segments and add transitional descriptions in between. 这个广告可以分为三段。两人或几人一组，根据这三段的内容设计对话。并在三段之间加上衔接的句子。

Segment 1: 0:04-0:06
Segment 2: 0:10-0:23
Segment 3: 0:37-0:44

Step 2: In turns, act out the dialogues along with the video in class. 在课上轮流边放视频边表演对话。

Instructional Strategies:

The instructor can play the video, pause at the end of each of the three segments, and lead the entire class to brainstorm first. Then the instructor can play the video again and pause at the end of each of the three segments, so each group takes turns to add and perform their dialogues.

Option 3: Creating a Sequel 拍续集

The advertisement only has 44 seconds. Now you would like to shoot a sequel with more conversations between the boy and the girl. Please compose the dialogue and act out your sequel. You may refer to the following checklist for designing your sequel. 这个广告只有44秒，现在你想拍续集，加上更多男孩子与女孩子的对话。请你和同学扮演不同的角色，把续集演出来。你可以用下面的清单帮助自己设计对话。

Checklist

1. WH-Word Information

I have included information about WHEN. YES NO
I have included information about WHO. YES NO
I have included information about WHERE. YES NO
I have included information about WHAT. YES NO
I have included information about WHY. YES NO

2. Language Use

I have checked use of words and vocabulary. YES NO
I have checked use of grammatical structures. YES NO

3. Creativity

I have fully explored my imagination and creativity to complete the task. YES NO

4. Effort

I have made effort to complete the task. YES NO

Instructional Strategies:

1. To create suspension and an "aha" moment while watching the commercial, the instructor should cover up the title of the commercial, i.e., 麦当劳—杨千嬅—薯条万万岁—雪地里的火车, so that the students have no idea of how the story line develops or concludes.

2. Being able to tell a story reflects language proficiency at the advanced level, but the ability to create a dialogue through roleplaying reflects a lower level of language proficiency at the intermediate level. If students are asked to narrate a story, be aware of the organizational devices required at the beginning, middle, and the end to construct a story. Otherwise, be flexible and accept simply key story lines. A typical intermediate-level leaner needs time and teacher's scaffolding to develop the ability to elaborate and use transitional conjunctions to connect key actions.

Rubric for Presentational Speaking/Writing

A. WH-word Information
4 Includes all WH-word information and elaboration
3 Includes all WH-word information with some elaboration
2 Includes some WH-word information with little elaboration
1 Includes limited WH-word information

B. Language Use
4 Excellent
3 Very good
2 Good
1 In progress

C. Creativity
4 Content and lines being very creative
3 Content and lines being creative
2 Content and lines being somewhat repetitive
1 Content and lines lacking creativity

D. Effort
4 Great effort
3 Good effort
2 Acceptable Effort
1 Little or no effort

F. Delivery (Speaking Only)
1 Fluent with comprehensible pronunciation all the time
2 Good flow, mostly comprehensible, several pauses
3 Incomprehensible sometime, some pauses
4 Difficult to understand, many pauses

Chapter 4

Beauty and Esthetics   美学艺术

Unit 2: Bring Happiness Home   把"乐"带回家

Contributor: Miao-fen Tseng
Proficiency Level: Novice-High to Advanced-Low
Instructional Time: 4-5 hours
Can-Do Statements:

1. Students can comprehend and interpret a video on a family's celebration of Chinese Lunar New Year.
2. Students can engage in the discussion of the story line of the video.
3. Students can connect a string of simple sentences to compose a short story based on the plot of the video (Novice-High).
4. Students can narrate a story by connecting a string of sentences to compose a story based on the plot of the video (Intermediate).
5. Students can narrate a story at the paragraph level based on the plot of the video (Advanced-Low).

Task 1   A Video on Chinese New Year Celebration   新春贺岁片

Communicative Mode: Interpretive and Interpersonal

Step 1: Watch the following video clip about celebrating Chinese New Year. 请看一个新春贺岁的影片：

https://youtu.be/cnt76lHFcso

Step 2: Discuss the following questions in groups then share with the whole class. 和你的同学分组讨论下面的问题，然后和全班同学分享。

Instructional Strategies:
Instructors may choose from the following questions based on the students' proficiency levels and class time.

Questions for Novice-high learners:
1. 这个电影的名字里有"新春"两个字，说的是什么中国节日？

2. Pepsi Cola 的中文怎么说？ Lays 的中文怎么说？
3. 电影里的老人在哪儿工作？
4. 他们见面的时候，天气怎么样？是什么季节（jìjié, season）？
5. 这位老人想不想他的家人？新春的时候，她觉得怎么样？
6. 开始过年的时候，谁跟老人一起过年？他们在老人家吃什么？老人的儿子跟女儿开始的时候想回家？后来回家了吗？
7. 老人有几个儿子，几个女儿？他们小时候喜欢吃／喝什么？（大女儿：柳橙；二女儿：乐事薯片；儿子：百事可乐）
8. 老人的儿子跟女儿做什么工作？（拍照片，旅行，唱歌）他们为什么不能回家？
9. 谁让老人的儿子跟女儿回家了？老人对他们说了什么？（对儿子说：别想一口喝完；对大女儿说：你的乐事，回家吧；对二女儿说：给你！）
10. 老人过年的时候，骑自行车出去做什么？
11. 电影最后，老人的儿子在他家前面做什么？
12. 你觉得这部电影想告诉大家什么？请写 1-3 句话。
13. 你觉得这部电影怎么样？你喜欢这部电影吗？为什么？
14. 你看完这部电影以后，有什么感想？请至少用三个句子写下你的感想。

Questions for Intermediate learners:

1. 这个视频的题目有"贺岁片"这三个字，"贺岁片"是什么意思？中国人一般什么时候看这种影片？
2. 这个视频的题目是《把乐带回家》。"乐"是什么意思？
3. 电影里的老人做什么工作？（火车站长）
4. 年轻人在哪儿看到这位（个）老人？（我的目的地就是这里）
5. 他们见面的时候，天气怎么样？是什么季节（jìjié, season）？
6. 这位老人看到年轻人以后，请他做什么？为什么？（天气太冷，请他到老人家过夜）
7. 年轻人到了老人的家以后，老人请他吃什么？（吃饺子）
8. 老人的儿子跟女儿不能回家过年，他的心情怎么样？
9. 老人有几个儿子，几个女儿？他们做什么工作？（大女儿／摄影师／照相的人，二女儿不知道，儿子／明星／歌星／歌手／唱歌的人）
10. 老人的女儿跟儿子为什么不能回家过年？
11. 一个很特别的年轻人给老人的三个子女什么东西？他做了什么，让这三个人回家了？
12. 老人的女儿跟儿子看到／拿了年轻人给他们的东西以后，觉得怎么样？想到什么事？后来怎么样？
13. 这三个年轻人在家里过年的时候，跟爸爸说什么吉祥话？（大女儿：祝你大吉大利；二女儿：年年有乐事；儿子：百事可乐）
14. 这部电影想告诉大家什么／想表达什么主题？
15. 你看完这部电影以后，有什么感想？请至少用三个句子写下你的感想。

Questions for Advanced-low learners:
1. 这部电影的片名是什么？（《把乐带回家》）
2. 电影中有一位年轻人，他的目的地是哪里？他在电影中扮演什么角色？跟这家人有什么关系？为他们全家四口人做了什么？发挥了什么作用？结果如何？
3. 电影中，老人有三个子女，请描述这位老人和他三个子女的个性／性格、外貌和工作。电影最后的结局怎么样？
4. 电影的开头，银幕上出现了下面的句子：
"每个人都希望和快乐不期而遇，有趣的是，我们永远不知道它会在哪里等我们。"电影最后，银幕上出现了下面的句子："我们已经在回家的路上了，你呢？"
你觉得这部电影想表达什么主题？
5. 电影的片名是《把乐带回家》。你觉得电影中想表达的"快乐"是什么？从你的角度来看，你认为"快乐"是什么？

Task 2   Story-Telling   讲故事

Communicative Mode: Interpretive, Interpersonal, and Presentational

Step 1: Watch the video again, narrate the plot of the video section assigned to you and come up with a string of sentences in sequence to describe the plot. 请再看一遍影片，把分配给你片段用几句话叙述出来。

Step 2: Share your narration with the whole class, and add transitional sentences guided by the instructor. 和全班分享讨论你的段落叙述，在老师的指导下加上连接的句子。

Step 3: Organize all the scripts, add your comments and thoughts. 把你的叙述整理在一起，在故事中间或者最后加上你自己的评论。

Step 4: Practice telling the story with your partner. 和你的同学练习叙述整个故事。

Instructional Strategies:
1. Although novice-high learners are unable to use cohesive devices such as conjunctions as smoothly as intermediate and advanced-low learners, organizing responses to all questions chronologically is an effective strategy to help them put pieces of information together and turn simple discrete sentences into a string of sentences with added connectors.
2. The rubric for story narration for AP Chinese is targeted to the intermediate – advanced levels. However, using it to grade novice-high learners' story writing would be a good starting point as well. Being able to use connectors is a key indicator of intermediate-low proficiency level. This task would prepare the novice-high learners for the next level.

Suggested Structures:

……以前 / 以后，（就）……
……verb + 完 + object + 以后，（就）……
Action 1 的时候，Action 2
先……，然后再……，再……
后来，……
……于是，……
……，结果……
最后……

Task 3   Story-Writing   写故事

Communicative Mode: Interpretive, Interpersonal, and Presentational

Step 1: Write up your story based on the video. 根据视频内容和上一个任务中的讨论，写一个故事。

Instructional Strategies:
When grading the students' writing, instructors can incorporate peer review to enhance students' self-awareness and motivation in finding syntax errors.

Step 2: Conscious-Raising Activity 意识培养活动

Option 1: Review 1-2 essays composed by your classmates, circle the connective devices in their essays. Then discuss the use of these structures and reflect on your own essay. 读一两篇你的同学写的故事，并圈出分句当中、分句之间与句子之间所有的连接词。在老师的带领下，全班一起讨论圈出来的连接词。

Option 2: Review 1-2 essays composed by your classmates in which the connective devices were taken out by the instructor. Fill in connective devices based on your knowledge and discuss with the class about where to insert them and how to use them. 读一两篇你的同学写的故事，这些故事中的连接词已经被去掉了，请你试着填一填。然后和全班讨论应填在哪里、怎么用连接词。

Instructional Strategies:
It's highly recommended that a "conscious-raising activity" be added after Task 3's writing activity for classes at novice and intermediate levels. The activity is typical in a task-based classroom. It provides students an opportunity to learn from others and raises awareness of the appropriate use of connectors, conjunction words, and coherent and cohesive devices.

Chapter 4
Beauty and Esthetics 美学艺术

Unit 3   Designing Advertisements and Posters   广告海报设计

Contributor: Lee-Mei Chen
Proficiency Level: Intermediate-Low to Intermediate-Mid
Instructional Time: 6-8 hours
Can-Do Statements:

1. Students can understand and discuss the relationship between hieroglyphics and standard Chinese characters and appreciate them on the artistic level.
2. Students can discuss and appreciate some successful advertisements, create their own advertisements, and present to the class.
3. Students can discuss how a library can serve people, create their own library promotion posters, and give an oral presentation about their posters.

Task 1   Beauty of Chinese Characters   认识汉字的美

Communicative Mode: Interpretive and Interpersonal

Step 1: Watch the following videos about Chinese characters. 看下面介绍汉字的视频。

汉字的故事：美
https://www.youtube.com/watch?v=PUybM3P2Pi4
"美"字是由"羊"字（羊头连角的象形）和"大"字（一个伸展两手的人之象形）组成，画出一个头戴羊角头饰的男人。羊角是公羊的武器，亦为强壮和男子气的象征，而按古代中国人的观念，一个"美丽"的男人应该是强壮和有男子气的。

汉字的故事：人
https://www.youtube.com/watch?v=9BzL9OR-BtQ
"人"字的原型为一个弯着身子两手合起来打招呼的人，人与万物的最大分别，在于人知规矩，知道何谓"应该"和"不应该"。

汉字的故事：月
https://www.youtube.com/watch?v=2AnSsQoh8Dg

除了月亮外，"月"字还有月份的意思，这是因为按照中国的农历，一个月的长短是依照月亮的"朔"（月亮被地球的影子完全遮盖，天上无月）和"望"（满月）而定。

Step 2: Watch the following video, write down the 36 Chinese characters you see from the video. 看下面的视频，写出你在视频里看到的36个汉字。

https://www.youtube.com/watch?v=kapOXVPozqc

Instructional Strategies:

The teacher may lead the class discussion. A prize will be awarded to students who write the most characters.

Step 3: Look at the logos below, discuss how the logo design uses the beauty of Chinese characters. 看一看下面的商标，说一说这些商标是怎么把汉字的美融入商标设计中的。

http://www.pmskill.net/
topic/5c7014baac63e61961666b4c

http://www.nipic.com/
show/3/82/7966382k620a45ef.html

102

https://kknews.cc/design/z582p5p.html https://k.sina.com.cn/article_2811490621_pa793f13d02700hvql.html

https://k.sina.com.cn/article_2811490621_pa793f13d02700hvql.html https://kknews.cc/design/z582p5p.html

https://k.sina.com.cn/article_2811490621_pa793f13d02700hvql.html https://k.sina.com.cn/article_2811490621_pa793f13d02700hvql.html

Step 3: Decide what kind of business the above logos represent, and fill in the following blanks. 根据上面的商标，想一想这些商标代表的是什么商店，并填写下面的表格。

你想买茶叶送人。	
你想买一些水果醋来喝。	
你想去参观古代的字画。	
你想买客厅沙发的垫子。	
肚子饿了，去哪儿吃？	
你想学习书法。	

Task 2   Designing Advertisements   广告设计

Communicative Mode: Interpretive, Interpersonal, and Presentational

Step 1: Look at the following advertisements that have Chinese characters. 看一看下面有汉字的广告。

104

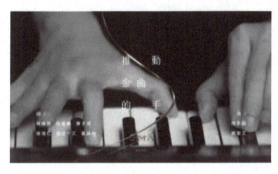

（图片来源自网络）

Step 2: Discuss whether the advertisements above are effective and eye-catching. Discuss what types of vocabulary can be used in advertising. 和你的同学说一说，上面的广告效果好不好？吸引人吗？在广告中可以用什么样的词语？

Instructional Strategies:
The teacher may guide the students to pay attention to the language used in the advertisements:
广告中的语言：
1. 精简为主
2. 少而不多言
3. 念起来有力
4. 以重点来思考
5. 能抓住人们的眼球

Step 3: In pairs, create an advertising poster using selected topics (like 保险、手机……) from a recent lesson, then present to the class. 两人一组，选一个最近学过的主题，设计一张广告海报，然后跟全班报告。

Suggested Structures:
我们设计的广告是……中最……
这是……，……什么都有，连……
……不但有……，而且有……，更重要的是……

Samples:

Task 3　Designing a Library Poster　设计图书馆宣传海报

Communicative Mode: Interpersonal and Presentational

Step 1: Discuss with the whole class about the reasons why fewer people go to the library now. 和你的同学讨论为什么人们越来越少去图书馆了。

Instructional Strategies:
The instructor can help lead the discussion or select a student to lead if needed.

Step 2: Work in pairs to design a poster with the following elements. 两人一组，设计一个海报，请包含下面的内容。
(1) Welcome sentences; (2) Library floor map; (3) Upcoming activities; (4) The library address, website, telephone number, library hours of operation

Step 3: Each pair present the poster in class. 每组同学展示设计的海报。

Samples：

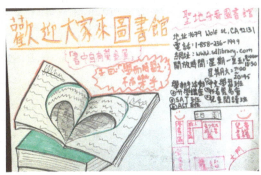
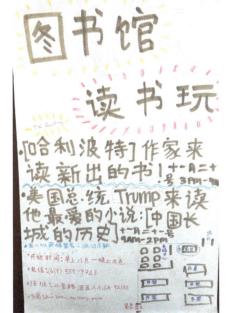

Rubric for the Design and Presentation

	4	3	2	1
Presentation	Creative, appealing, enriched Chinese symbolic culture and essence, accurately and neatly written	Interesting, strong token of Chinese culture, appropriately written	Meaningful, some token of Chinese culture, appropriately written	Uninteresting, lacking Chinese culture, inappropriately written
Layout	Well-organized, easy to follow, eye-catching, variegated, appealing	Organized, smooth, with mixed colors, interesting	Somewhat organized, with mixed colors, plain	Simple, disorganized, difficult to follow, uninteresting
Content	Inclusive, expressive, excellent combination of language and cultural difference	Appropriate and good combination of language and cultural difference	Fair combination of language and cultural difference	Incomplete, insufficient information and cultural difference
Language	Accurate and rich vocabulary and idiomatic expressions, neatly written characters	Appropriate vocabulary and some idiomatic expressions, intelligibly written characters	Somewhat inappropriate vocabulary, some unintelligibly written characters	Mostly inappropriate vocabulary, unintelligibly written characters
Expression	Two take equal turns, no transitional silence or interruptions, familiarity with content, clear presentation, frequent eye contact with the audience	Two take equal turns, few transitional silence or interruptions, familiarity with content and few hesitations, clear presentation, frequent eye contact with the audience	One member takes more time than the other, noticeable transitional silence and interruptions, hesitations with content, infrequent eye contact with the audience	Two take unequal turns, many transitional silence and interruptions, no familiarity with content, little or no eye contact with the audience

Chapter 4

Beauty and Esthetics 美学艺术

Unit 4: Advertisements in the East and the West 东西方文化对广告的影响

Contributor: Lee-Mei Chen
Proficiency Level: Intermediate-Mid to Intermediate-High
Instructional Time: 4-5 hours
Can-Do Statements:

1. Students can interpret McDonald's advertisements and discuss cultural similarities and differences reflected on McDonald's products in China and the U.S.
2. Students can understand and comprehend articles about pizzas, discuss cultural similarities and differences in China and the U.S., and express their opinions about food localization.
3. Students can interpret and analyze Coca-Cola commercials and discuss similarities and differences in cultural practices and perspectives in China and the U.S.
4. Students can develop intercultural awareness of Chinese and American advertisements and design a video advertisement of a drink.

Task 1   Fast Food in China and the U.S.   中美快餐店的差异

Communicative Mode: Interpretive, Interpersonal, and Presentational

Part 1: Beverages 饮料

Step 1: Look at the two advertisements below and discuss the similarities and differences of products available in China and in the U.S. 看一看下面的两个广告，和你的同学讨论。

Step 2: Select your answer below, then write two sentences to answer the questions in the next row. 填写下面的表格。选择之后请用两句话解释说明。

Required linguistic components to incorporate in the sentence descriptions:

Conjunctions: 却有，却没有，还有，可是

Adverbs: 也，都

Frequency adverbs: 常常，有时候，不常

Other key words: 一般来说……，喜欢/爱……，认为……，……比……，我觉得……

	中国	美国
饮料的大小	☐ 大杯的多 ☐ 小杯的多 ☐ 大小不是重点，可以自由选择 1. 2.	☐ 大杯的多 ☐ 小杯的多 ☐ 大小不是重点，可以自由选择 1. 2.

(续表)

	中国	美国
有热汤吗	☐ 有热粥 ☐ 有玉米浓汤 ☐ 没有	☐ 有热粥 ☐ 有玉米浓汤 ☐ 没有
	1. 2.	1. 2.
冷饮多还是热饮多	☐ 冷饮多 ☐ 热饮多	☐ 冷饮多 ☐ 热饮多
	1. 2.	1. 2.
冷饮上面加奶油吗	☐ 几乎都加奶油 ☐ 不加奶油 ☐ 自由选择加或不加	☐ 几乎都加奶油 ☐ 不加奶油 ☐ 自由选择加或不加
	1. 2.	1. 2.
冰咖啡的种类	☐ 很多 ☐ 比较少	☐ 很多 ☐ 比较少
	1. 2.	1. 2.
水果做的冷饮	☐ 有而且很受欢迎 ☐ 没有	☐ 有而且很受欢迎 ☐ 没有
	1. 2.	1. 2.
茶做的饮料	☐ 有 ☐ 没有	☐ 有 ☐ 没有
	1. 2.	1. 2.

Step 3: Discuss your answers with the whole class. Pay special attention on cultural differences. 和全班讨论你的答案。请特别注意文化差异。

Step 4: Conduct the survey below on two friends, one with Chinese background and one with American background to find out the cultural differences. Then report your findings to the class. 请你给来自中国家庭和美国家庭的两个朋友做下面的调查问卷，看一看有什么文化差异。然后向全班报告你的调查。

饮料	中国人家庭	美国人家庭	补充或附加说明
早餐时喝的饮料	☐冰 ☐热 ☐常温	☐冰 ☐热 ☐常温	
午晚餐时喝的饮料	☐冰 ☐热 ☐常温	☐冰 ☐热 ☐常温	
口渴时喝的饮料	☐冰 ☐热 ☐常温	☐冰 ☐热 ☐常温	
生病时喝的饮料	☐冰 ☐热 ☐常温	☐冰 ☐热 ☐常温	
运动完喝的饮料	☐冰 ☐热 ☐常温	☐冰 ☐热 ☐常温	

Part 2: Pizza 比萨饼（披萨）

Step 1: Read the following articles, then fill in the blanks.
为什么国内的 Pizza 普遍比美国的好吃？
https://www.zhihu.com/question/22407472
意式披萨 v.s 美式披萨
https://www.douban.com/note/508052499/

	意大利	美国	中国
饼皮			
基本的酱及奶酪			
馅料			
文化因素（为什么会有不同）			

Step 2: Discuss the following questions. 讨论下面的问题。

1. 许多餐饮业者为了适应当地人的饮食文化习惯，会将外国食物变得"本土化"一些，这样做有什么好处？
2. 你是否同意以下看法：我们的食衣住行等各方面的生活习惯传到其他国家以后，都有可能产生改变而适应当地的生活模式。请举例说明。

Task 2   Differences Between Chinese and U.S. Coca-Cola Advertisements   中美可口可乐广告的不同

Communicative Mode: Interpretive, Interpersonal, and Presentational

Step 1: Watch the following videos. 看下面两个视频。
http://www.youtube.com/watch?v=TSmHcN8nLuo

https://www.youtube.com/watch?v=RY1pcizCKT8

Instructional Strategies:
1. The teacher needs to understand why there are different characters in these two advertisement videos. The Eastern version uses two movie stars to catch people's eyes and the Western version uses diversity to show Coke is the common beverage.
2. The advertisement videos' backgrounds are very important. The Eastern version

showing Coke is a beverage for affluent population. The display at the Western version is a drink that everyone can drink anytime, anywhere.
3. Storing the Coke in a cooler versus in a backpack also shows the cultural differences.
4. The end of these two videos: the Eastern version shows the round cap, which signifies the concept of reunion. The Western version shows the shape of the bottle implying keeping your body in shape.

Step 2: Complete the following worksheet. 填写下面的表格。

问题	美国影片	中国影片
他们两人在哪儿见面？	☐街上任何角落 ☐高级且多人出入的场所	☐街上任何角落 ☐高级且多人出入的场所
男孩的可乐放在哪儿？		
男孩和女孩各穿什么衣服？	☐轻松舒服的平时服装 ☐漂亮、高级的外出服装	☐轻松舒服的平时服装 ☐漂亮、高级的外出服装
你觉得男孩喜欢女孩吗？为什么？		
那时的天气怎么样？和可乐有关吗？		
两个广告选在不同的季节，有什么特别的意义吗？		
这两个广告有哪些相同的地方？		
这两个广告有哪些不同的地方？		
为什么美国影片里的人物是不同种族的普通人，而中国影片里的人物是电影明星？		
你认为最后的镜头，一个是瓶身一个是瓶盖，有特别的意义吗？是什么？		
你认为这两个广告要表达什么？		

Step 3: Discuss your answers with your classmates. 和你的同学讨论你的答案，然后向全班报告。

Step 4: Discuss the questions below. 和你的同学讨论下面的问题。

1. 你认为找名人拍广告推销产品好吗？为什么？
2. 如果广告结束的时候不用瓶身和瓶盖作结尾，你会怎么做来显示出东西文化的不同？
3. 成功的广告一定要深入人心，你认为这两个广告是否达到了这样的效果？
4. 若这两个可乐广告的男女对话重新改写，你会怎么改？为什么？
5. 如果由你来设计东西文化不同的饮料广告，你会怎么做？

Step 5: Work with two of your classmates, design and shoot a video advertisement for a drink. The video should be no more than 2 minutes. 和你的两位同学一起设计并拍摄一个饮料的广告。广告要在两分钟以内。

Rubric for the Video Presentation

	4	3	2	1
Overall Presentation	Creative, appealing, enriched culture comparison and essence, accurately and neatly perform	Interesting, strong token of culture difference, appropriately performed	Meaningful, some token of culture difference, appropriately performed	Uninteresting, lacking culture difference, inappropriately performed
Layout	Well-organized, easy to follow, eye-catching, variegated, appealing	Organized, smooth, with colors, interesting	Somewhat organized, with colors, plain	Simple, disorganized, difficult to follow, uninteresting
Content and Information	Inclusive, expressive, excellent, showing the cultural difference	Appropriate and good, showing the cultural difference	Fair, showing the cultural difference	Incomplete, insufficient information and cultural difference
Spoken Language	Accurate and rich vocabulary and idiomatic expressions, neat sentences	Appropriate vocabulary and some idiomatic expressions, intelligible sentences	Somewhat inappropriate vocabulary, some unintelligible sentences	Mostly inappropriate vocabulary, unintelligible sentences
Oral Expression	No transitional silence or interruptions, familiar with content, clear presentation	Few transitional silence or interruptions, familiar with content and few hesitations, clear presentation	Noticeable transitional silence and interruptions, hesitations with content	Many transitional silence and interruptions, no familiarity with content

Chapter 4

Beauty and Esthetics 美学艺术

Unit 5: My Room and Chinese Feng Shui 卧室中国风

Contributor: Miao-fen Tseng
Proficiency Level: Intermediate-Low to Intermediate-High
Instructional Time: 8-10 hours
Can-Do Statements:

1. Students can describe their bedrooms, the layout of furniture and relevant information, and share comments.
2. Students can understand colors and numbers and their symbolic meanings in Chinese culture.
3. Students can understand and interpret Feng Shui taboos for the layout of a bedroom in Chinese culture, exchange ideas and opinions, and present their thoughts and perspectives.
4. Students can discuss what they have learned with parents, gather their parents' comments and perspectives, propose an improvement plan for better Feng Shui and present the layout of their newly designed bedrooms.

Task 1   My Bedroom 我的房间/卧室

Communicative Mode: Interpretive, Interpersonal, and Presentational

Step 1: Take a few pictures of your room, bring them to class to share with your classmates. Then introduce your room based on the structure below. 照几张你房间的照片，带到教室来分享给大家看，然后根据下面的描述准备一段话来介绍你的房间。

报告内容：
1. 基本信息
   这个房间是在公寓里还是房子里？一个人住吗？有没有室友？什么时候开始住在这里的？
   为什么要住在这儿？很贵吗？方便吗？安静吗？离学校近吗？附近环境怎么样？一个月租金是多少？为什么？

2. 设备
   有什么设备？设备怎么样？新不新？为什么？
3. 家具摆设
   房间里有什么家具？还有什么其他的东西？它们摆在哪儿？请介绍家具的形状、大小、颜色和摆放的位置。家具的上下左右有什么东西？请描述一下这些东西。
4. 装饰品
   房间里有什么装饰品？墙上贴着什么？挂着什么？书桌上放着什么？摆着什么？地板上有什么？这些东西对你有什么特别的意义？
5. 喜好与建议
   你喜欢这个房间吗？为什么？
   你对这个房间满意吗？对哪些方面满意？对哪些方面不满意？怎么样才会让你更满意？
6. 总结
   请用一到三句话总结。

Step 2: In groups, introduce your room to each other. The audience may ask questions. 全班分成几个小组，组员之间互相介绍自己的房间，互问互答。

Step 3: In front of the whole class, each student takes turns to introduce his or her room. When presenting, the audience take notes and prepare to ask the presenter questions and answer the teacher's questions. 每个同学再轮流介绍，其他同学一边听，一边做笔记，准备提问，同时也回答老师问题。

Instructional Strategies:
1. The task above is used as a review activity that leads to the following core tasks to develop the key concepts of Chinese Feng Shui. Students should have learned the existential structures and be given the opportunity to incorporate these skills to complete the series of tasks below.
2. Remember to convert the speaking task to a writing task that is necessary to consolidate and cycle learning to conclude Task 1. To create a writing rubric, simply remove the last two categories specific for speaking and add general writing conventions or any special writing requirements that are appropriate for your students. The speaking task can precede the writing task or vice versa.

Suggested Structures:
Place + PW + verb +（着）+ MW + noun
黑板　　　上　　　有　　　　　　一些　　字。

桌子	旁边	是	一本		书。
床	前	坐着/站着	一个		人。
书桌	后面	放着/摆着	一把		椅子。
墙	上	挂着	一幅		书法/画。
地	上	堆着	很多		衣服。
门/墙	上	贴着	一张		海报。

PW: position word
MW: measure word

Rubric for Oral Presentation

I. Comments and Opinions

4 Includes a variety of comments on the room such as likes and dislikes, interesting anecdotes, opinions about the room, reaction to the placement of the furniture, etc.

3 Includes some comments on the room such as likes and dislikes, interesting anecdotes, opinions about the room, and reaction to the placement of the furniture, etc.

2 Includes few comments on the room such as likes and dislikes, interesting anecdotes, opinions about the room, and reaction to the placement of the furniture, etc.

1 Includes almost no comments on the room such as likes and dislikes, interesting anecdotes, opinions about the room, and reaction to the placement of the furniture, etc.

II. Existential Sentences and Fundamental Structures

4 Shows accurate use of existential sentences and fundamental structures except for occasional errors

3 Shows accurate use of existential sentences and fundamental structures with several consistent errors

2 Shows some accurate use of existential sentences and fundamental structures with some consistent errors

1 Shows frequent inaccurate use of existential sentences and fundamental structures

III. Rich Vocabulary and Expressions

4 Uses rich vocabulary and expressions
3 Uses appropriate vocabulary and expressions
2 Uses some vocabulary and expressions
1 Uses limited vocabulary and expressions

IV. Tones and Pronunciation

4 Tones and pronunciation are accurate, with no or minimal errors that do not impede comprehension

> 3 Tones and pronunciation are generally accurate, with sporadic errors that do not impede comprehension
> 2 Some tones and pronunciation are generally inaccurate, with consistent errors that impede comprehension
> 1 Many tones and pronunciation are most of time inaccurate, with consistent errors that impede comprehension
>
> **V. Fluency**
> 4 Speaks at a natural and smooth pace, with occasional pauses and hesitation
> 3 Speaks at a smooth pace, with some repetition, pauses, and hesitation
> 2 Speaks at a slow pace; struggles with meaning; has quite a few repetition, long pauses and hesitation
> 1 Speaks at a very slow pace; frequently struggles with meaning; has many repetition, pauses, and hesitation

Task 2　What Does Color Represents?　颜色象征什么意义？

Communicative Mode: Interpretive and Interpersonal

Step 1: Look at the following pictures and discuss why red and yellow are the two main representative colors in Chinese culture and what they represent. Compare with the U.S. culture or your own culture. 看下面的图片，讨论为什么红色和黄色是中国的代表色，并讨论这两种颜色在美国文化里的象征意义，进行中美文化对比。如果你有其他文化背景，也请讨论一下。
（The following photos are selected from **https://zhuanlan.zhihu.com/p/31061920**）

Step 2: Answer the following questions guided by the instructor. 在老师的带领下回答下面的问题。

1. 你是否听过"风水"这个词？"风水"有什么意义？代表什么中国文化传统？
2. 颜色跟风水有什么关系？对风水有什么影响？能改善风水吗？
3. 你最喜欢什么颜色？为什么？这些颜色在美国或你自己的国家有什么象征意义？

Step 3: Study on the following article, then answer the questions and discuss in groups. 全班一起讨论学习下面这篇文章，然后回答下面的是非题，最后分组讨论答案。

室内装修使用的色彩影响住宅的风水，红色在中国是最受欢迎的颜色，表示吉利、好运与喜庆。比如说，"生意红红火火"；"一个人红得发紫"；过年的时候，会发红包、写春联、穿红色的衣服。

黄色是高贵、权威、长寿的象征。故宫中的服饰及宫殿装修的主色调都使用金黄色和朱红色，以表示高贵与权威。

绿色代表生命、活力与希望，是室内装修中常用的色调，室内配以绿色地毯和盆景，会使人心平气和。但是，中国人对绿色有一个忌讳，你在中国几乎找不到绿色的帽子。如果一个男人"戴绿帽子"，就是说他的太太有外遇了。

白色和黑色，表示悲哀和死亡。按中国人的生活习惯，尽量不用黑色、纯蓝、深灰、中灰、纯白等颜色。

（The above article is revised from 家居风水：色彩与风水的关系？99%的人不知道 http://www.sohu.com/a/157554738_449070 ）

判断对错：
1. 中国人最喜欢红色。
2. 红红火火表示生意做得很成功，赚很多钱。

3. 红得发紫是指一个人非常有名。
4. 中国过年的时候，一定看得到红色。
5. 黄色象征尊贵与地位。
6. 绿色在中国都是正面的意思。
7. 绿帽子在中国很受欢迎。
8. 在中国，白色与黑色的代表意义与美国不同。
9. 一般来说，一间风水很好的卧室不常看到白色和黑色。
10. 在中国文化中，颜色的选择跟风水有很大的关系。

Step 4: Read the following article, learn and discuss about the meaning of numbers in the U.S. and Chinese cultures. 读一读下面的文章，学习并讨论中美文化中对数字的偏好和意义。

https://baike.baidu.com/item/%E6%95%B0%E5%AD%97%E5%B4%87%E6%8B%9C

Instructional Strategies:
The instructor may prepare some pictures to help students understand the meaning of numbers.

数字崇拜

所谓数字崇拜，是指人们对某个数字或某些数字特别偏爱，认为这样的数字可以给自己带来好运气或避免晦气，能帮助自己或升官或发财，如中国的8、6、9、7和3等。这些人对数字的崇拜大多是由"字音"而来的，比如8的发音近似于"发"。数字崇拜现象在世界上很多国家都存在。与数字崇拜同时存在的，是数字避讳，而中国避讳最多的是4，因为它的发音近似于"死"，所以不吉利。西方人则避讳13。

Guided questions:
1. 中国2008年的奥运会是在几点几分几秒开始的？为什么？
2. 为什么中国很多电梯和大楼都没有第四层或四号？
3. 六六大顺是什么意思？跟哪个数字有关？
4. 长长久久是什么意思？跟哪一个数字有关？
5. 二在风水上有什么意义？请举几个跟二有关的例子。
6. 美国什么数字最吉利？什么数字最不吉利？为什么？
7. 其他问题？

Step 5: Guided by your instructor, learn and discuss the meaning of the numbers in the Temple of Heaven. Watch the following video, read the two articles and discuss the meaning of the numbers with your classmates, then complete the comprehension tasks. Report on 3-5 most interesting takeaways from learning about the Temple of Heaven. 在老师的带领下学习讨论天坛的数字与风水。先看下面的视频，读一读两篇文章，再讨论数字在中国建筑里的运用与象征意义，然后完成以下选择题。最后，每位同学轮流说出3～5点天坛让你们印象最深刻的部分。

https://www.bilibili.com/video/av49668786/?spm_id_from=333.788.videocard.4

https://m.88tph.com/sucai/12433367.html

第一篇文章

　　天坛的特殊性体现一个"天"字上。所以，建筑细节上处处体现为这个至高无上的"天"服务。

　　天坛圜丘的尺度和构件的数量集中并反复使用"九"这个数字，以象征"天"和强调与"天"的联系。

　　中国古代认为9为数之极，是最尊贵的象征，因此圜丘坛建筑与9关系极为密切。圜丘坛的中心是一块圆形大理石（称作天心石）。从中心面向外，3层台面每层都铺有9环扇面形状的石板，上层第1环为9块，第2环为18块，第3环为27块，到第9环为81块；中层从第10环的90块到第18环的162块；下层从第19环的171块到第27环的243块。3层总计378个9，共3402块，象征九重天。

　　祈年殿殿正中有4根高大的通天柱，象征一年有春、夏、秋、冬四季。中层有金柱 12 根，象征一年的 12 个月。外层的 12 根檐柱，象征一天的 12 个时辰。中、外层相加 24 根，象征一年的 24 个节令。三层相加共 28 根，象征周天二十八星宿。

（资料来源：天坛与数字 以"九"为尊典范 http://www.naic.org.cn/html/2018/gjfs_0428/42742.html ）

1. 天坛的建筑，处处都跟哪一个数字有密切关系？
   1）1　　　　2）3　　　　3）8　　　　4）9
2. 这个数字代表跟什么的联系？
   1）人　　　　2）神　　　　3）天　　　　4）地
3. 9 这个数字象征什么？
   1）权力　　　2）尊贵　　　3）升官　　　4）发财
4. 天坛的外观是什么形状？
   1）圆形　　　2）椭圆形　　3）方形　　　4）长方形
5. 圜丘坛有什么特色？
   1）一共有三层，二十七圈　　　2）最大的一圈一共有 243 个石块
   3）每一圈的石块都是 9 的倍数　4）以上皆是
6. 祈年殿使用什么样的柱子建造而成？
   1）圆柱　　　2）方柱　　　3）三角柱　　4）五角柱
7. 祈年殿里四根最大的柱子叫什么？代表/象征什么意义？
   1）龙井柱，四个季节
   2）金柱，四个季节
   3）檐柱（yánzhù），四个季节
8. 祈年殿里除了四根最大的柱子以外，还有几根圆柱？
   1）12　　　　2）18　　　　3）24　　　　4）36
9. 祈年殿里的金柱与檐柱分别代表什么意义？
   1）12 个月，12 个时辰　　　2）12 个时辰，12 个月
   3）12 个月，12 个月　　　　4）12 个时辰，12 个时辰
10. 祈年殿里一共有多少根柱子？
    1）24　　　　2）28　　　　3）32　　　　4）36

第二篇文章

https://wenku.baidu.com/view/bea5f5fdcf2f0066f5335a8102d276a20029609c.html?re=view

1. 天坛的外观是什么形状？
   1）圆形　　　2）椭圆形　　3）方形　　　4）长方形

2. 古代中国皇帝在天坛做什么？
   1）祈天祈福　　2）开会议事　　　　3）休闲避暑　　　　4）吟诗作乐
3. 祈年殿使用什么样的柱子建造而成的？
   1）圆柱　　　　2）方柱　　　　　　3）三角柱　　　　　4）五角柱
4. 祈年殿里四个最大的柱子，叫什么？代表／象征什么意义？
   1）龙井柱，四个季节
   2）金柱，四个季节
   3）檐柱（yánzhù），四个季节
5. 祈年殿里除了四个最大的柱子以外，还有几个圆柱？
   1）12　　　　2）18　　　　　　3）24　　　　　　4）36
6. 祈年殿里的金柱与檐柱分别代表什么意义？
   1）12个月，12个时辰　　　　2）12个时辰，12个月
   3）12个月，12个月　　　　　4）12个时辰，12个时辰
7. 祈年殿里一共有多少根柱子？
   1）24　　　　2）28　　　　　　3）32　　　　　　4）36
8. 圜丘坛有什么特色？
   1）一共有三层，二十七圈
   2）最大的一圈一共有243个石块
   3）每一圈的石块都是9的倍数
   4）以上皆是
9. 以下哪一个词代表皇帝至高无上的地位？
   1）五九之尊　　2）九五之尊
   3）尊之九五　　4）尊之五九
10. 天坛的建筑，处处都跟哪一个数字有密切关系？
   1）1　　　　　2）3　　　　　　3）8　　　　　　4）9

Additional source: 天坛建筑透露的数字玄机"九""五"因何被皇家推崇？
http://www.sohu.com/a/210689454_229863

Instructional Strategies:
The above two sets of multiple-choice questions were generated from two online articles that share a lot of similar information. They are complementary to each other and therefore are listed here for teachers to choose according to their preferences.

Task 3　Taboos of Bedroom Feng Shui　卧室的风水禁忌

Communicative Mode: Interpretive and Interpersonal

Step 1: Jigsaw. Divide the class into 4-6 groups, each group becomes the expert group of 2-3 illustrations below. They read the sections of the 2-3 taboos and then share the information with the whole class. Thus the whole class builds a complete picture of the entire text. 全班分成4～6组，每一组负责解释2-3个图，轮流带领大家学习。

各组需要完成的任务是：
1. 根据图文，告诉大家每一个图所代表的禁忌。
2. 根据图文，告诉大家每一个图可能会对健康产生的不良影响。
3. 总结自己组内的观点，讨论哪些禁忌是合理的，哪些禁忌是不合理的，并说明理由。

Instructional Strategies:
1. Encourage each group to use 百度翻译 (**https://fanyi.baidu.com**) for independent learning and generating a personal vocabulary list prior to their oral presentation.
2. Ask each group to create a PowerPoint file and make sure that new words and expressions are listed at the bottom of each PowerPoint slide ensure peer's comprehension.
3. Make the vocabulary list readily accessible to all students. Distribute a handout to the entire class or upload it to a Google Drive or any language management system; i.e., online course site.

卧房风水禁忌
1. 房门不可以对厕门

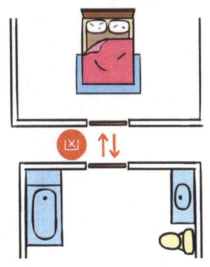

　　房门对到厕所门，会造成病痛及钱财流失。厕所是湿气、臭气、秽气产生的地方，如果房门对到厕所门，刚好全部接收。

2. 厕所门不可以对床

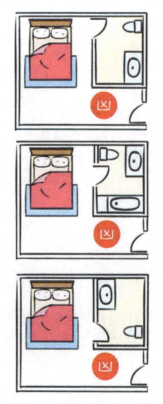

房间里的厕所对床，情况比房门对到厕所更严重，对到头，会头痛、思考时不能集中；对到腰，会腰酸、心脏无力，住久了会产生糖尿病、心脏病；对到脚，会坐骨酸痛、膝盖无力，住久了会产生意外骨折。

3. 镜子不可以对床

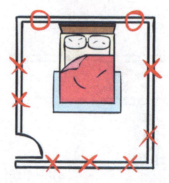

镜子对床，会造成精神不佳，不能集中。卧室里除了床头两边可以放镜子以外，其他位置都不可放。但是，如果在衣柜里面加一面镜子，平时关着的时候看不到，是很好的设计，放在什么位置都可以。

4.床上不可以有横梁

　　睡在横梁下,大脑或心脏会直接受到负面影响,造成睡眠不足、头痛等现象。建议在梁下放矮柜,或干脆作整面包梁立顶柜来避开。

5.床位不可以在楼梯下方

　　床在楼梯下方,睡在床上的人,睡眠状况一定不会好,经常噩梦不断。运势也非常差,很难有翻身的机会。

6.床头隔墙不可以对马桶

　　头顶着马桶睡觉,会造成思考无法集中和头痛的问题。

129

7.床头要靠实墙

　　有些人为营造气氛而将床斜放，不靠墙。床头不靠实墙或调头睡，会造成睡眠品质不良、思想叛逆、行为怪异及与人沟通能力不良。

8.床前不可以有电视机、音响、手机

　　房间里有电视机必然会产生两种情况：一、长期躺在松软的床上，易造成脊椎弯曲变形。二、容易躺在床上看电视，忍不住会多看一两个节目，直到非常困了才肯睡，因此搞得每天睡眠不足，长期下来，事业、健康定会出问题。另外，现代人常在睡觉时仍开着手机，并把手机放在床头，对健康非常不利。

9.床位不可以在空调下方

　　把床位放在空调下方，冷空气不断吹向头、肩、颈，加上人在睡眠状态时，毛细孔会略微放开，轻者经常感冒，重者会造成头、肩、颈的神经紧张、肌肉僵化。
　　睡觉的位置上或下是厕所，有多恶心不用解释也想得到，只是一般人只想到自家空间如何充分利用，忽略了楼上、楼下的关系。另外如果床的楼上或楼下是厨房炉灶，会让人肝火过旺，影响肝功能。

10. 天花板上不可以有华丽的大吊灯

　　床位上方不可挂奇形怪状的灯具，会使人产生紧张不安的感觉。在地震频发的当今，床的正上方最好是完全没有任何灯具。

The photos and descriptions above are slightly modified based on the following source.
"不得不看的卧房风水禁忌"
https://towner4896.blogspot.com/2013/11/blog-post_6264.html?view=flipcard

Step 2: Based on the 10 illustrations above, think about your own bedroom. Have you violated any of the taboos? Complete the chart below by checking items and provide reasons. 根据以上10个卧室风水禁忌图，想一想自己的卧室有没有触犯一些中国风水的禁忌？请完成下面这张表格，在适当的格子里打"√"，并说明原因。

禁忌	我的卧室触犯这个禁忌了吗？	这个禁忌合理吗？为什么？
1. 房门不可以对厕门		
2. 厕所门不可以对床		
3. 镜子不可以对床		
4. 床上不可以有横梁		
5. 床位不可以在楼梯下方		
6. 床头隔墙不可以对马桶		
7. 床头要靠实墙		
8. 床前不可以有电视机、音响、手机		
9. 床位不可以在空调下方		
10. 天花板上不可以有华丽的大吊灯		

表格统计

1. 我的卧室一共触犯了_____个中国风水禁忌。
2. 以上卧室的10个禁忌中，我认为不合理的禁忌有_____个，理由是_____。
3. 从中国的风水来看，我卧室的风水_____很好_____不错_____不好。

(Circle the one that best reflects your own evaluation.)

Instructional Strategies:

1. The link on page 133 that shows bad Chinese bedroom Feng Shui lists more than 10 taboos. The above table has selected only 10 taboos that are considered more interesting from the perspectives of young American learners. Feel free to add or remove items that suit discussion in your class.

2. Chinese Feng Shui has gained its popularity in Western societies. It has long-standing traditions and legacies in Chinese culture although some concepts about Chinese Feng Shui may be considered superstitious. It's important for teachers to lead students to understand how Chinese Feng Shui connects with Chinese people's daily life and surroundings, and how it conforms with logic and science. A simple topic on one's bedroom is a great start to trigger learners' interest in this regard, but it counts on teachers to guide students to apply the concepts of Chinese Feng Shui to improving the quality of their life.

3. In general, parents are more concerned about the arrangement of furniture and facilities at home than their children. This unit has chosen the bedroom for focal discussion assuming teenagers and college students are more interested in talking about their own bedrooms rather than living rooms or kitchens. That's why it might be worth involving parents to know what their children have learned at school, hoping their children can share some concepts of Chinese Feng Shui with their parents, and if possible, take actions to re-arrange the placement of some furniture if they see fit.

Step 3: In pairs, exchange information from your completed chart using the questions below. Take notes of your partner's answers. 两个人一组，互相交换信息，用下面的问题，互问互答，把你同学的答案记下来。

1. 你的卧室触犯了几个禁忌？是哪几个禁忌？你觉得这些禁忌合理吗？为什么？
2. 你卧室的风水好不好？你对你卧室的风水满意吗？
3. 这几个禁忌对你的健康造成影响了吗？除了健康以外，还有什么其他方面的影响？
4. 你想进一步改善你卧室的风水吗？你认为可以怎么做？
5. 你认为这些风水禁忌是迷信还是科学？跟人们的心理感受及对环境的判断有什么关系？
6. 你打算怎么告诉你的爸爸妈妈？会建议怎么改？

Task 4 How to Change Bedroom Feng Shui?
如何改善卧室的风水？

Communicative Mode: Interpretive and Interpersonal

Step 1: Discuss how to change Feng Shui in your bedroom based on the video you watched in class. Then present to the class. 先看以下一段视频，然后和你的同学讨论如何改善卧室风水，再向全班同学报告。

Instructional Strategies:

The instructor may choose from the following videos according to students' interests.

"摆对床位了吗？"
https://www.youtube.com/watch?v=cHkh7tklKkY

"招惹小人的床头摆设？（加屏风）"
https://www.youtube.com/watch?v=qSP0Hjz5q88

"什么是散魄的房间"
https://www.youtube.com/watch?v=mQFn7I9UB6U

"常生病与房间电视有关？"
https://www.youtube.com/watch?v=n0sHzBH4vQM

Step 2: Discuss bedroom Feng Shui with your parents: tell your parents what you have learned in Chinese class about color, numbers, and Feng Shui. Show them the ten pictures about bedroom Feng Shui taboos and help them understand what kind of arrangement may benefit Feng Shui in bedrooms. Ask them to sign below the form. 与爸妈讨论如何改善卧室风水：回家以后，告诉爸爸妈妈你在中文课学到的中国文化里颜色、数字、风水的知识。请把10张卧室风水禁忌图拿给他们看，让他们了解中国卧室里的东西要怎么摆设才会有好风水。请他们看过你的表格以后，在表格的最下面签名。

讨论题目：颜色、数字、卧室的风水

说明：我们已经学了在中国文化里，颜色、数字和卧室的风水所代表的意义。请跟你的爸爸妈妈分享你所学到的知识，以及课堂讨论的内容，完成下面的表格，然后请父母签字。

学生姓名：
讨论日期：
爸爸或妈妈姓名：
1. 颜色在中国文化里的象征意义 　　红色 　　黄色 　　绿色 　　黑色 　　白色
2. 数字在中国文化里的象征意义 　　最吉利的数字 　　最不吉利的数字 　　最喜欢和最不喜欢的数字
3. 卧室的风水 　　1）你的卧室触犯了几个中国风水的禁忌？ 　　2）你认为这些禁忌合理吗？ 　　3）你爸妈认为这些中国风水的禁忌合理吗？为什么？ 　　4）跟爸妈讨论，你们打算怎么改善卧室的风水？ 　　5）如果你们根据这些禁忌做了一些改变，请照几张照片，带来教室给同学们看，准备一个简短的口头报告。 　　6）其他意见

爸爸或妈妈签名：_____

Task 5　Bedroom with the Best Feng Shui　谁的卧室风水最好？

Communicative Mode: Presentational

Scenario: you are a very popular designer. Now you have a proposal to redesign an old bedroom. You would like to use the latest designing concepts with the implementation of Chinese cultural elements and participate in a competition. You are very confident that you will win this competition. Prepare a presentation for the new design ideas. 假设你是一个很红的设计师，你现在拿到一个企划案，要给一个旧的卧室改头换面，用最新的设计理念，把现代中国风带入卧室设计，参加一个"中国风卧室设计比赛"，你认为你很有希望得奖，为了这个设计比赛，你正在准备一个公开说明会。

Step 1: After learning about Feng Shui taboos, redesign the bedroom by adding Feng Shui concepts and Chinese cultural elements. 了解风水禁忌以后，根据风水重新设计卧室，并帮卧室增加中国风的元素。

Step 2: Design a slideshow and report the changes you have made and what your new bedroom looks like. 设计 PPT，用卧室的照片告诉大家你做了哪些改变，现在这间卧室变成了什么样。

时间长短：5-6 分钟
报告方式：PPT＋口语报告
报告内容
1. 描述改变以前的卧室。
2. 原来的卧室触犯了哪些风水禁忌？对你有什么不好的影响？你对哪些方面很满意或不满意？
3. 你决定做哪些改变？为什么？请从中国风水的角度来解释，包括大小、颜色、形状、摆设等等，说明中国文化中代表的象征意义，并加上自己个人的喜好。
4. 准备报告的时候，自己再上网多多了解中国卧室传统。以下是一个可以参考的网站，除此之外，也鼓励学生自己上网找找。
卧室中国传统：https://cn.dreamstime.com/%E5%9B%BE%E5%BA%93%E6%91%84%E5%BD%B1-%E5%8D%A7%E5%AE%A4%E4%B8%AD%E5%9B%BD%E4%BC%A0%E7%BB%9F-image21753232

Step 3: After all the presentations, vote for the best design. 全班同学报告以后，投票评选谁是最佳中国风的卧室设计师。

Suggested Structures:
我对 + somebody/something +（不）满意
我想 / 可以 / 得 / 应该把 something 变成 / 换成 / 做成 / 漆成 + something
我想 / 可以 / 得 / 应该把 color 深 / 浅一点
我想 / 可以 / 得 / 应该把 size 变大 / 小 / 长 / 短 / 宽 / 窄一点
我想 / 可以 / 得 / 应该把 shape 变一点
大小
把……变……一点
　　　大 / 小 / 长 / 短 / 宽（kuān, wide）/ 窄（zhǎi, narrow）
颜色
把……变……一点
　　　浅 / 深 / 暗 / 亮 / or add a color name
颜色 / 物品
把……换成……
　　　改成
　　　漆成
　　　变成
形状
把　　方的 / 长方形的　　换成 / 变成 / 改成　　圆的 / 椭圆的

Rubric for Oral Presentation

	4	3	2	1
Powerpoint Organization	Well-organized, clear layout, almost no typos, well-chosen visual aids such as photos or images	Organized, good layout, a few typos, appropriate visual aids such as photos or images	Somewhat organized, acceptable layout, some typos and visual aids	Disorganized, unclear layout, many typos, insufficient visual aids
Information & Content	Relevant, accurate, elaboration of ideas and perspectives, sufficient evidence of full understanding of Chinese cultural elements in Feng Shui	Relevant, mostly accurate, with some progression of ideas and perspectives, some evidence of understanding of Chinese cultural elements in Feng Shui	Partially relevant and accurate information, plain descriptions lacking development and progression of ideas and perspectives, insufficient evidence of understanding of Chinese cultural elements in Feng Shui	Information mostly irrelevant and inaccurate, little elaboration of ideas and perspectives, limited evidence of understanding of Chinese cultural elements in Feng Shui
Language Use	Excellent use of existential sentences and sentences indicative of change in colors, size, shape, placement of furniture, and their symbolic meanings; rich vocabulary, phrases, and idiomatic expressions	Appropriate use of existential sentences and sentences indicative of change in colors, size, shape, placement of furniture and their symbolic meanings; appropriate use of vocabulary, phrases, and idiomatic expressions	Limited appropriate use of existential sentences and sentences indicative of change in colors, size, shape, placement of furniture and their symbolic meanings; limited appropriate use of vocabulary, phrases, and idiomatic expressions	Many inappropriate use of existential sentences and sentences indicative of change in colors, size, shape, placement of furniture and their symbolic meanings; inappropriate use of vocabulary, phrases, and idiomatic expressions
Fluency & Confidence	Frequent eye contacts, no or little reliance on written notes, almost no pauses or hesitation, smooth delivery indicative of confidence and excellent preparation	Some eye contacts, no or little reliance on written notes, few pauses or little hesitation, smooth delivery indicative of confidence and sufficient preparation	Few eye contacts, reliance on written notes, pauses or hesitation, delivery indicative of some confidence and preparation	No eye contacts, a lot reliance on written notes, many pauses or much hesitation, delivery lack of confidence and preparation

Instructional Strategies:
The development of speaking and writing go hand in hand. To follow up with the speaking task delineated in the above rubric, it is necessary to ensure the development of writing skills. To turn the above rubric to be suited for writing, simply remove the last category of Fluency & Confidence and add writing conventions such as the number of characters and paragraphs required, punctuation, typos, etc. Be reminded to balance between handwriting and typing and avoid heavy or complete reliance on typing.

Task 6   Cultural Presentation   文化报告

Communicative Mode: Presentational

Step 1: Feng Shui has lasting influential impact on how Chinese people think, live, and do in their daily life. Describe your understanding of this cultural heritage, its significance and impact on Chinese life, such as famous architecture, scenic spots, historical sites, home and its surrounding, interior design, furniture placement, and so on. 风水的理念对中国人的思想、生活和日常行为都有很大影响。请你描述一下你对这个文化传统的理解，包括它在著名历史建筑、风景名胜、居家、室内设计、家具摆设等各个方面的重要性和影响。

Rubric: Refer to the scoring guidelines for cultural presentation in speaking for AP Chinese.

其他参考资料
百科卧室风水
https://baike.baidu.com/item/%E5%8D%A7%E5%AE%A4%E9%A3%8E%E6%B0%B4

卧室风水这样做 夜夜好眠不是梦
http://www.jiajumi.com/know/Feng Shui/8645.html

中国颜色
http://www.chineseteachers.com/blog/resource_content.jsp?id=115

Chapter 4

Beauty and Esthetics   美学艺术

Unit 6: Chinese Historical Courtyard Homes (Siheyuan)   中国的四合院

Contributor: Lee-Mei Chen
Proficiency Level: Intermediate-High to Advanced-Low
Instructional Time: 8-10 hours
Can-Do Statements:
1. Students can understand what Siheyuan is.
2. Students can learn from the appearance of the "门当","户对","门环" in ancient times to understand the size of the official residence of the family.
3. Students can understand the culture and art of Siheyuan.
4. Students can understand the design of the modern Siheyuan.
5. Students can understand that today's courtyard house still has its advantages in architecture.
6. Students can compare the Siheyuan house designs of East and West styles.
7. Students can understand and interpret rental advertisements of Siheyuan in China.
8. Students can understand and discuss what to focus on when selecting from different Siheyuan for living.

Task 1   Historical Courtyard Homes   了解古代的四合院

Communicative Mode: Interpretive, Interpersonal, and Presentational

Step 1: Read the article below, then discuss the following questions. 读下面的文章，和同学讨论相关问题。

https://history.ifeng.com/c/7oLxx5rh8oE

Instructional Strategies:
The instructor may teach a song about the Chinese dynasty before this task.
https://www.youtube.com/watch?v=3wCSPj7SlEk

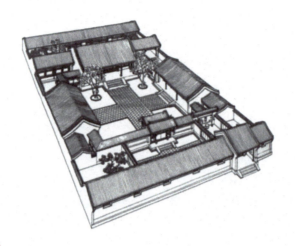

一、"院"是什么？

1. "院"指的是什么？
2. "庭院"指的是什么？
3. "庭院"与"院子"有什么不同？
4. 中国最早的庭院是哪一朝的宫殿建筑？

（Answers：1. 最初指的是墙围起来的空地。2. 现在表示建筑和墙体围起来的、人们用于生活的空地。3. 我们日常理解的院子其实是后来与"庭"合称的"庭院"。4. 夏朝的宫殿建筑。）

二、四合院从哪里来？

1. 中国最早的四合院是在哪一个时期出现的？
2. 中国最早的四合院有几个院子？这些院子是如何分配来使用的？
3. 为什么说东汉时期的四合院形式十分丰富？
4. 魏晋与隋唐时期的四合院，已经是主流住宅，我们可以从哪儿找到证明？
5. 宋元两代四合院的前堂后室，都用什么来连接？
6. 我们见过的四合院形式基本在哪一个朝代定型？

（Answers：1. 现知我国最早的四合院是在西周时期出现。2. 最早的四合院已有了前后两个院子，四周房屋围合，前院正房为前堂，用于宴会和礼仪。后院的是后室，用作主人的日常起居。东西两侧的房子给其他家庭成员居住。3. 由东汉画像砖中的合院，可以看出，房子和廊子围合、大门偏西，东院还有高高的望楼，可见这时的合院建筑形式十分丰富。4. 魏晋与隋唐时期的四合院已是主流住宅，形式更加丰富，在敦煌壁画中可以看见。5. 这时的四合院前堂后室多用工字型廊子连接。6. 明清时，四合院高度成熟，每个地域形成了自己鲜明的风格，我们见过的四合院形式也基本在这个时候定型。）

三、北京四合院有多少种？

1. 什么是"进"？什么是"跨"？

2. 什么是一进院、二进院、三进院？

3. 什么是东跨院、西跨院？

4. 什么是一进四合院（单进四合院）、两进四合院、三进四合院、四进或以上的四合院？

5. 中国四大名著中的《红楼梦》里主角之一的贾母，住的是哪一种四合院？

6. 多跨的四合院，其实各个跨院彼此是独立的，那跨院之间是如何连通的？

（Answers：1. 前后方向院子的个数叫"进"。院子的个数叫"跨"，就是横着"跨"。2. 前后方向院子，你进几个门，就叫几进院。所以进一个门叫一进院，进两个门叫二进院，进三个门叫三进院。3. 四合院的正院往西边跨一步就叫"西跨院"；正院往东边跨一步，就叫"东跨院"。4. 四合院只有一个院子、只进一个大门，叫一进四合院或单进四合院。有两个院子，需要进两个门，因此叫两进四合院。有三个院子，需要进三个门。在前院，内院的基础上加了一个后院，因此叫三进四合院。四进、五进甚至七进的四合院，都是在三进四合院的基础上将三进四合院的一个内院变为多个内院，前后院不变。5.《红楼梦》中地位崇高的贾母住的就是五进四合院。6. 多跨四合院的各跨院彼此独立，但会在跨院墙上开小门连通。）

四、四合院里的房子

1. 四合院里的大门，指的是哪里？一般在院子里的哪个角落？

2. 大门在八卦中的巽（xùn）位，有什么特别的意义吗？

3. 什么是四合院里的倒座房？在四合院里倒座房和其他房子的不同是什么？是给谁住的？

4. 什么是垂花门？

5. 俗语说："大门不出，二门不迈。"二门是指哪一个门？

6. 什么是正房、厢房？各是给谁住的？

7. 什么是耳房？是做什么用的？

8. 回廊有什么用处？

9. 四合院的最后一座建筑叫什么？通常是给谁使用的？

10. 何时是后罩楼的高峰期？

（Answers：1. 四合院里的大门，一般是在院子的东南角。2. 大门的位置是风水八卦中的巽位，这是个生财的位置。3. 倒座房是院里唯一一座，背向街道的房子，是院落最外侧的一座。也可以说它是倒着坐的一座房子，因此得名"倒座房"；倒座房一般是给用人或者外来的客人住宿用。4. 两进以上的四合院里才会出现"垂花门"，它是宅子的第二进门，因门上的垂莲柱而得名。5. 俗话说的"大门不出，二门不迈"，二门指的就是垂花门。6. 正房一般是内院正中的建筑，是宅子中等级最高的建筑，屋顶也高于其他建筑。正房是供主人使用，一般是一家之主居住在内。厢房位于内院两侧，一般是有两座厢房正对，厢房是给主人的儿子及儿媳居住使用。7. 耳房位于正房两侧，好似正房的耳朵而得名。耳房一般较小，一般用作贮藏室。8. 回廊就好像人在冬天把手臂揣进袖子，抄起双手一样，因此叫"抄手游廊"。

人可以在回廊下避雨、休息。9. 后罩房是四合院的最后一座建筑，它是四合院的收尾，将整个宅子罩住，后罩房位于后院，有最好的私密性，常常给女眷使用，偶有情况给用人使用。10. 家财较为丰厚的主人也会将后罩房建为二层，称其为"后罩楼"。清末民国时期是后罩楼建设的高峰期。)

五、院里的"小物件"

1. 常放在大门的前后两侧或者二门（又叫_____）的前后两侧，叫_____，又叫门鼓石、抱鼓石，又叫门档、门当。

（Answers：垂花门，门墩石）

2. 四合院的影壁有两种，一种是放在进入大门迎面的墙上，叫_____；另一种是设在门外，与大门相对，中间隔着胡同。还有比较高级或官员的门口，像个"八"字形打开，叫_____（或撇山影壁）。

（Answer：照壁，八字影壁）

3. 在门框、门楣上可以看到两个或四个的砖雕或木雕叫_____（或户对）。

（Answer：门簪）

http://blog.sina.com.cn/s/blog_819174960102z3oh.html

http://blog.sina.com.cn/s/blog_9e2b39570102uw95.html

Step 2: Watch the video below from the beginning to 0:56, then discuss with your classmates about what you see in the video. 看下面的视频到56秒，然后和你的朋友讨论你看到的内容。

https://www.youtube.com/watch?v=VX4_SNv3kzU

Step 3: Read the following article and answer the questions. 读下面的文章，回答问题。

https://zhidao.baidu.com/question/4332535.html

1. 什么是"门当"？什么是"户对"？
2. 为什么每户人家的门当和户对都不一样？
3. 你觉得"门当"、"户对"有什么好处？
4. 现在延伸的"门当户对"是什么意思？

（Answer：1."门当"原指大宅门前的一对石鼓，又叫抱鼓石。"户对"是置于门楣上或门楣双侧的砖雕、木雕。2.文官的家用圆形的"门当"，武官的家用方形的"门当"，所以大老远一看，就可知道这家的主人是文官还是武官。"户对"用短圆柱形，是代表了古人重男丁的观念，意在祈求人丁兴旺。3."户对"的大小与官品职位的高低成正比。古时三品以下官宦人家的门上有两个门当，三品的有四个，二品的有六个，一品的是八个，只有皇帝的皇宫才能有九个，取"九鼎之尊"之意。4.门当户对：是指夫妻（或未婚男女）之间的家庭背景相仿，或家庭背景在社会中的影响力相当，称为门当户对。）

https://zhidao.baidu.com/question/4332535.html

143

http://blog.sina.com.cn/s/blog_819174960102z3oh.html

Step 4: Continue watching the video below till 1:34, discuss what you see in the video. 继续看视频到1分34秒，和你的朋友讨论看到的内容。
https://www.youtube.com/watch?v=VX4_SNv3kzU

Step 5: Watch the following video, then fill in the form and answer the related questions. 看下面的视频，然后填表并回答问题。
https://v.qq.com/x/page/a0029s01xv9.html

Instructional Strategies:
After watching, ask the students to read the passage below to determine if they understood.

新年的时候，很多人家都要挂春联、贴门神，这都是来自上古的桃符（Táofú）。东汉时期，有两个兄弟，一个叫神荼（Shén Tú）一个叫郁垒（Yù Lěi），住在山上的桃树下，如果有鬼来，他们就用绳子绑起来去喂老虎。因为传说鬼比较怕桃木，后来的人们就用他们的头像或名字刻在桃木上，然后放在门上驱邪避鬼（qū guǐ bì xié）。后世改用纸张，叫桃符；也有用绘画的，就是门神。

桃符的另一种形式是写上文字，就是写上神荼和郁垒两人的名字；随着文学的发展，两句带有吉祥的对仗句子（duìzhàng jùzi），就成了今日的春联。

对仗句子：对仗句是用字数相等、结构形式相同、意义对称的一对短语或句子来表达两个相对或相近意思的修辞方式。当然，要两面对称不能多字也不能少字。如：

　　春回大地风光好
　　福满人间喜事多

http://blog.sina.com.cn/s/blog_706a16ca0102yhk8.html

新年的时候，中国人家家户户门上贴着什么？	□春联　□门神　□财神爷
新年的时候，中国人家家户户门的两旁贴或挂着什么？	□春联　□门神　□财神爷
新年的时候，中国人家家户户挂春联、贴门神是为什么？	□漂亮　□驱邪避鬼　□招财进宝
新年的时候，中国人家家户户挂春联、贴门神，这是来自上古的什么？	□图画　□桃符　□传说
中国的传说里，鬼怕哪一种木头？	□桧木　□桃木　□一般的木头
春联对仗句子的形式	□字数相等、结构相同　□不受拘束
春联对仗句子的内容	□自由书写　□意义对称的吉祥短语或短句

1. 请说说门神是如何从桃木、桃符变成的？
2. 春联是怎么来的？有什么特别的形式？
3. 你觉得贴门神、挂春联有什么好处？

Step 6: Continue watching the video below till 2:02, talk with your classmates about what is "门环". 继续看视频到 2 分 02 秒，说一说什么是门环。

https://www.youtube.com/watch?v=VX4_SNv3kzU

门环，又叫响器，是装在房屋大门上的拉手，也是给人叩门用的，中国门环也常被称为铺首或门钹，但铺首和门钹只是门环不同形式的底座。门环常以金属制成，在中国古代有严格的等级规定。

叩门（kòu mén）：knock（on the door/gate）

门环（mén huán）、铺首（pù shǒu）、门钹（mén bó）：knocker，和现在的门铃类似

底座（dǐzuò）：base

Step 7: Watch the video below till 4:33, then fill in the following chart. 看视频到 4 分 33 秒，然后填写下面的表格。

https://www.youtube.com/watch?v=VX4_SNv3kzU

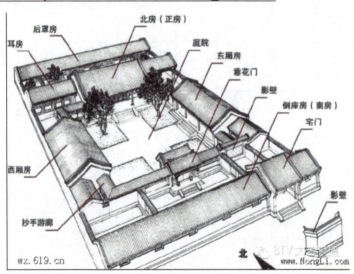

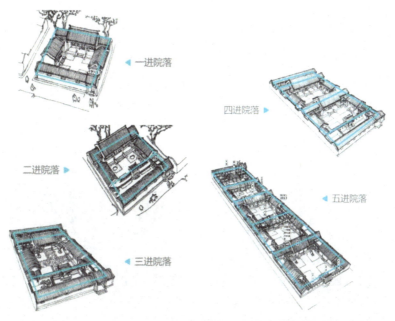

	四合院	一般现代中国人住的公寓和房子
占地的大小	☐ 大 ☐ 小	☐ 大 ☐ 小
庭院的数目	☐ 多 ☐ 少	☐ 多 ☐ 少
院子里圆形拱门的数目	☐ 多 ☐ 少 ☐ 没有	☐ 多 ☐ 少 ☐ 没有
院子里回廊的数目	☐ 多 ☐ 少 ☐ 没有	☐ 多 ☐ 少 ☐ 没有
窗户的设置	☐ 多 ☐ 少 ☐ 围墙上也有	☐ 多 ☐ 少 ☐ 围墙上也有
外面的人容易看到里面吗？	☐ 容易 ☐ 不容易	☐ 容易 ☐ 不容易
大门上有门当和户对吗？	☐ 都有 ☐ 都没有	☐ 都有 ☐ 都没有
院子里庭院空间	☐ 很隐秘 ☐ 开放	☐ 很隐密 ☐ 开放
建筑格局	☐ 注重传统尊卑等级 ☐ 平等	☐ 注重传统尊卑等级 ☐ 平等

Step 8: Draw a picture of the Siheyuan then write a paragraph/paragraphs to describe Siheyuan. 画一幅四合院的图，然后写一段 / 几段话描述四合院。

147

Students' sample works:

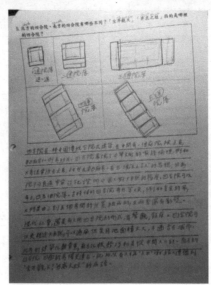

Instructional Strategies:
Prep reading for teachers:
http://www.ddove.com/news/214.html 中国传统四合院
http://uschinews.com/20180122/1188 中国的四合院才是真正的豪宅
https://kknews.cc/culture/5x9zkyk.html 中国四合院的详细图解，满满都是文化
https://kknews.cc/history/k8bq5rb.html 四合院有什么好处？以前的人为什么要这样建？

Rubric for Writing

	4	3	2	1
Organization	Including opening, middle and ending	Somewhat including opening, middle and ending	Not clear on opening, middle and ending	No opening, middle or ending
Vocabulary	The author uses vivid words and phrases. The choice and placement of words seems accurate, natural, and not forced.	The author uses vivid words and phrases. The choice and placement of words is inaccurate at times and/or seems overdone.	The author uses words that communicate clearly, but the writing lacks variety.	The writer uses a limited vocabulary. Jargon or clichés may be present and detract from the meaning.
Sentence, Structure, Grammar, Mechanics and Spelling	All sentences are well-constructed and have varied structure and length. The author makes no errors (or very few) in grammar, mechanics, and/or spelling.	Most sentences are well-constructed and have varied structure and length. The author makes a few errors in grammar, mechanics, and/or spelling, but they do not interfere with understanding.	Most sentences are well-constructed, but they have a similar structure and/or length. The author makes several errors in grammar, mechanics, and/or spelling that interfere with understanding.	Sentences sound awkward, are distractingly repetitive, or are difficult to understand. The author makes numerous errors in grammar, mechanics, and/or spelling that interfere with understanding.
Elaboration	Thoughts are fully articulated and the content shows that Siheyuan is carefully studied.	Thoughts are somewhat addressed and the content shows that Siheyuan is studied.	Thoughts are incompletely addressed or unaddressed and the content shows that Siheyuan is somewhat studied.	Lack of thoughts and ideas, the content shows that Siheyuan is not studied.

Task 2   Modern Courtyard Homes   现代的四合院

Communicative Mode: Interpretive, Interpersonal, and Presentational

Step 1: Read the following two articles. 读下面两篇短文。
https://kknews.cc/zh-my/geomantic/r3pr3yo.html
https://tuzhizhijia.com/gaifangzhishi/12593.html

Step 2: Work in pairs, discuss and fill in the following chart. 和你的同学一起讨论完成下面的表格。

	现代的四合院	传统的四合院	我们的看法
楼层	☐ 单层 ☐ 两层或以上 ☐ 有阁楼	☐ 单层 ☐ 两层或以上 ☐ 有阁楼	
空间	☐ 大 ☐ 不一定大，但是充分利用空间来设计	☐ 大 ☐ 不一定大，但是充分利用空间来设计	
卧室	☐ 注重尊卑的位阶 ☐ 注重家庭成员的居住隐私 ☐ 卧室有独立小院 ☐ 二楼开窗注重不对视	☐ 注重尊卑的位阶 ☐ 注重家庭成员的居住隐私 ☐ 卧室有独立小院 ☐ 二楼开窗注重不对视	
厨房	☐ 旧式阴暗通风不良 ☐ 现代明亮注重干净 ☐ 舒适的餐厅 ☐ 餐桌是圆桌 ☐ 注重视野	☐ 旧式阴暗通风不良 ☐ 现代明亮注重干净 ☐ 舒适的餐厅 ☐ 餐桌是圆桌 ☐ 注重视野	
采光	☐ 明亮、通风 ☐ 方便就好，不注重亮光	☐ 明亮、通风 ☐ 方便就好，不注重亮光	
屋顶	☐ 加高，注重采光 ☐ 注重质材优、美观耐用 ☐ 注重传统的形式	☐ 加高，注重采光 ☐ 注重质材优、美观耐用 ☐ 注重传统的形式	
质材	☐ 建造质材更先进，可以防水、防风、挡冷热 ☐ 以木材、石头为主	☐ 建造质材更先进，可以防水、防风、挡冷热 ☐ 以木材、石头为主	
大门	☐ 注重中国式的流线 ☐ 注重风水的方位	☐ 注重中国式的流线 ☐ 注重风水的方位	
庭院	☐ 不种在坟地常见的松树、柏树、杨树 ☐ 种枣树（早生贵子）、柿树（事事如意） ☐ 种丁香、海棠表示主人有身份及文化修养	☐ 不种在坟地常见的松树、柏树、杨树 ☐ 种枣树（早生贵子）、柿树（事事如意） ☐ 种丁香、海棠表示主人有身份及文化修养	
其他	☐ 加建车库、健身房、娱乐房	☐ 加建车库、健身房、娱乐房	

Step 3: Read the following article, then write a short paragraph to answer the guided questions. 读下面的文章，然后写一段话回答问题。
http://www.huaxia.com/zt/2001-23/60507.html

1. 如果有机会，你想住四合院吗？为什么？
2. 你认为住四合院有什么好处？
3. 如果你有一笔钱买房子，在一栋四合院和一栋豪华别墅之间，你会选哪一间？为什么？

Instructional Strategies:
Prep readings for the teachers:
https://kknews.cc/zh-cn/history/k8bq5rb.html 四合院有什么好处？以前的人为什么要这样建？

文章重点内容如下：
四合院至少有以下5个优点：

一、单层建筑接地气：
　　传统四合院都是单层的，可能受限制于当时的结构技术，也可能是因为古代中国没有人口压力和土地的限制，总之老祖宗们选择了居住在地面。接地气，对身体健康有益。

二、坡屋顶引导自然风进入院内：
　　当时的结构技术只允许做坡屋顶，而坡屋顶上空的风，却因为屋顶的引导而向下进入院子内部，一部分沿另一个坡屋顶向上走，一部分则进入檐口以下的院子内部。

三、建筑和庭院良好的围合关系：
　　西方的居住建筑更多的是在场地中央建起一栋独立的建筑，建筑被院子所包围。中国刚好反过来，是在场地周围建起房子，院子被包围在中间，形成了典型

的庭院式建筑，这个差别是两种文化、两种思维方式的差别，各有所长，并无优劣之分。

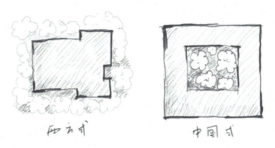

四、房间的等级和空间的递进层次：

　　四合院遵循着一大堆的"规则"，从外到里，从低到高，男女、长幼、主仆，都是儒家的那一套。我倒不是说要坚持传统四合院的所有规则，我只强调规则本身，有规则一定比没规则更适合中国。

　　西方的小住宅建筑所遵循的规则就很少，整个流线从外面到里面，唯一的目的就是"到达"，家庭成员之间的差别和空间的递进层次是没有关系的，只体现在主卧和次卧的面积大小上面。所以我们就发现中西住宅不同的流线关系：

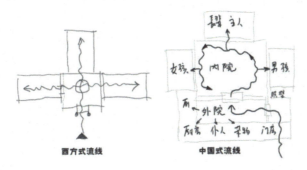

五、精美的装饰性元素：

　　传统四合院有大量的装饰性元素可供借鉴，贝聿铭的苏州博物馆也在尝试着用现代结构技术去概括传统的建筑装饰元素。如下图，贝大师居然想出用钢和玻璃模仿古时候的瓦屋顶和斗拱，相当精练和传神。

Rubric for the Short Paragraph

	4	3	2	1
Organization	The content is clear all; the three requirements are included.	The content is clear; two requirements are included.	Not clear on content; two requirements are included.	Not clear on content; one requirement is included.
Vocabulary	The author uses vivid words and phrases. The choice and placement of words seems accurate, natural, and not forced.	The author uses vivid words and phrases. The choice and placement of words is inaccurate at times and/or seems overdone.	The author uses words that communicate clearly, but the writing lacks variety.	The writer uses a limited vocabulary. Jargon or clichés may be present and detractd from the meaning.
Sentence, Structure, Grammar, Mechanics and Spelling	All sentences are well-constructed and have varied structure and length. The author makes no errors in grammar, mechanics, and/or spelling.	Most sentences are well-constructed and have varied structure and length. The author makes a few errors in grammar, mechanics, and/or spelling, but they do not interfere with understanding.	Most sentences are well-constructed, but they have a similar structure and/or length. The author makes several errors in grammar, mechanics, and/or spelling that interfere with understanding.	Sentences sound awkward, are distractingly repetitive, or are difficult to understand. The author makes numerous errors in grammar, mechanics, and/or spelling that interfere with understanding.

Task 3　Rent a Siheyuan　租个四合院

Communicative Mode: Interpretive and Interpersonal, and Presentational
Scenario: Mark and his three friends will go to China to study Chinese for one year. He has 2,000 dollars' budget for rent. Since Mark started learning Chinese, he has been fascinated by its culture, especially its architechture. He could appreciate the beauty and greatness of Chinese culture from traditional Chinese buildings. He has convinced the others to stay in a Siheyuan and has been researching on an appropriate one to stay while he's in China. Below are three Siheyuan he has found. 马克和朋友共四人，将从美国去中国学中文一年，手上每个月有两千美金的房租预算。从开始学中文起，马克就很喜欢中华文化，特别是传统的建筑，他觉得传统的建筑里，可以看到中华文化的古色古香、中华文化的美丽及伟大，甚至可以走入中国历史；他说服了其他三人同意一起住四合院，所以他在网上寻找出租的四合院。下面是他找到的三个四合院。

（1）北京东城四合院出租 会所接待 画室 工作室

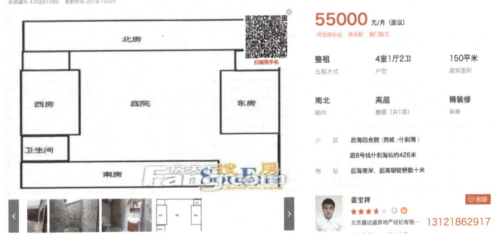

房源描述

房源亮点
院落坐落：150平米
建筑面积：120平米
房屋格局：15南15北15东15西
院落布局：正房厢房
停车情况：附近停车场
装修情况：精装修
地理：二环内主城区，名胜古迹，商超医院
环境：胡同干净整齐
签约年限：可谈

	周边配套	大学：东方财经日语大学
		中：柳荫街、西城区建业培训
		机构：文化部、中国民用航空总局机关、北京市公安局
		商场：顺达杂货店、北京市老东方家具城
		邮局：中国邮政
		银行：中国建设银行西四支行德胜储蓄所
		医院：中道堂中医门诊部、北京门诊部
		其他：北京航鑫园宾馆、积水潭旅馆

	交通出行	公交：55路 地铁：2号线、4号线、6号线、8号线

配套设施

床　　宽带　　电视　　冰箱　　洗衣机　　空调　　热水器　　暖气

微波炉　　可做饭　　卫生间　　沙发　　衣柜　　阳台　　电梯

（2） 北新桥簋街四合院 钥匙房 全采光地下 地暖新风空调　　　分享　收藏

房源编号 437715402　更新时间 2019-09-21

116700 元/月（面议）

整租	4室3厅4卫	650平米
出租方式	户型	建筑面积
南	高层	精装修
朝向	楼层（共1层）	装修

小　区　后海四合院（西城 / 什刹海）
　　　　距8号线什刹海站约426米
地　址　后海南岸，距离银锭桥数十米

常镜超
★★★★
北京丽兹行房地产顾问有限…
从业信息卡　营业执照

房源描述

- **房源亮点**
  - 占地：308平米
  - 地下：308平米（全采光地下室）
  - 露台：50平米
  - 房况：精装修，带地暖，新风，空调
  - 年租金：140万
  - 看房：钥匙房随时看

- **周边配套**
  - 其他：北京航鑫园宾馆、积水潭旅馆

- **交通出行**
  - 公交：55路
  - 地铁：2号线、4号线、6号线、8号线

配套设施

 床　 宽带　 电视　 冰箱　 洗衣机　 空调　热水器　暖气

电梯

（3）北京东城四合院出租 自主 景山公园 恭王府附近

房源描述

房源亮点
院落坐落：100平米
建筑面积：90平米
房屋格局：15南15北15东15西
院落布局：正房厢房
停车情况：附近停车场
装修情况：精装修
地理：二环内主城区，名胜古迹，商超医院
环境：胡同干净整齐
签约年限：可谈

周边配套
大学：东方财经日语大学
中：柳荫街、西城区建业培训
机构：文化部、中国民用航空总局机关、北京市公安局
商场：顺达杂货店、北京市老东方家具城
邮局：中国邮政
银行：中国建设银行西四支行德胜储蓄所
医院：中道堂中医门诊部、北京门诊部
其他：北京航鑫园宾馆、积水潭旅馆

交通出行
公交：55路地铁：2号线、4号线、6号线、8号线

配套设施

床　宽带　电视　冰箱　洗衣机　空调　热水器　暖气
微波炉　可做饭　卫生间　沙发　衣柜　阳台　电梯

Step 1: This coming weekend, Mark and his friends will get together to discuss which one for rent is better. Students work in pairs to fill in the blanks and help Mark gather all needed information before meeting her friends.

这个周末，马克他们四人将聚在一起讨论选哪一个四合院比较好。请你和你的同学讨论后填写下面的表格，帮马克和他的朋友想一想应该选哪个四合院。

	北京东城会所接待	北新桥簋街附近	北京东城景山公园附近	建议
户型				
建筑面积				
高层				
配套设施				
交通				
停车场				
租金				
其他				
不清楚处				
补充				

Step 2: After each pair presents their completed table in class, the instructor leads the entire class to discuss the results, elicit more thoughts and opinions, and enter information in the following table.

各组报告以上步骤完成的表格，由老师带领全班集体讨论，将讨论的结果填入下表，完成统计，最后宣布结果，决定哪一间四合院最适合。

四合院	赞成	原因	不赞成	原因
第一间				
第二间				
第三间				
补充